W9-AVY-930

The New York Times

POCKET
MBA
SERIES

FORECASTING BUDGETS
25 KEYS TO SUCCESSFUL PLANNING

NORMAN MOORE, PH.D.
University of Connecticut

Lebhar-Friedman Books
NEW YORK • CHICAGO • LOS ANGELES • LONDON • PARIS • TOKYO

For *The New York Times*
Mike Levitas, Editorial Director, Book Development
Tom Redburn, General Series Editor
Brent Bowers, Series Editor
James Schembari, Series Editor

Lebhar-Friedman Books
425 Park Avenue
New York, NY 10022

Published by Lebhar-Friedman Books
Lebhar-Friedman Books is a company of Lebhar-Friedman Inc.

Printed in the United States of America

Library of Congress Cataloging-in-Publication Data
On file at Library of Congress
ISBN 0-86730-776-5

DESIGN & PRODUCTION BY MILLER WILLIAMS DESIGN ASSOCIATES

Visit our Web site at lfbooks.com

Volume Discounts

This book makes a great human resources training reference.
Call (212) 756-5240 for information on volume discounts.

INTRODUCTION

LEBHAR-FRIEDMAN BOOKS is proud to present *The New York Times* Pocket MBA Series, 12 invaluable reference volumes that are easily accessible to all businesspersons, from first level managers to the executive suite. The books are written by Ph.D.s who teach in the MBA programs in some of the finest schools in the country. A team of business editors from *The New York Times*—Mike Levitas, Tom Redburn, Brent Bowers, and James Schembari—provided their own expertise to edit a reference series that is beyond compare.

The New York Times Pocket MBA Series offers quick-reference key points learned in top MBA programs. The 25-key structure of each volume presents an unparalleled synopsis of crucial principles of specific areas of business expertise. The unique approach to this series packages academic books for consumers in an easy-to-use trade format that is ideal for the individual businessperson as well as an excellent training reference manual. Be sure to get all 12 titles in the series to complete your own MBA education.

Joseph Mills
Senior Managing Editor
Lebhar-Friedman Books

25 KEYS TO SUCCESSFUL PLANNING

CONTENTS

KEY 1

Budget blues

L et's face it. Producing a budget is often a very unpleasant task. Why? There are several explanations. First, the budgeting process is often a stand-alone exercise. The various units prepare their budgets in isolation with no input or guidance from upper management or other departments that might affect future operations.

Second, the budget is perhaps the most important output generated by the firm's planning process. But if upper management does not outline the firm's goals and objectives and develop a business plan, it will be difficult for middle and lower level managers to develop budgets to achieve those goals and objectives. Third, budgets are themselves plans for the future. Like all plans, they require specifying and estimating relevant assumptions and forecasts. Forecasting the future is generally a difficult and unpleasant task. The future is a moving target and a proper budget should reflect that uncertainty or risk. Fourth, budgets are used to monitor and control operations and activities. The budget process must generate a blueprint that is able to distinguish between controllable and uncontrollable events. Fifth, budgets are based on accounting data and are expressed in financial terms. Many managers have no formal accounting training and have a great deal of difficulty in understanding the accounting requirements involved in preparing a budget. Finally, the budget process is time consuming. Volumes of worksheets and computer spreadsheets must be prepared and reconciled.

If the budgeting process is so costly, difficult and time consuming, why bother? Because a good budget is critical to your firm's success. Companies need a method to link business plans—mission statements, strategies, objectives, and tactics—with the firm's actual activities. This is the role of the budget process. In return, the budgeting process provides a mechanism for keeping track of costs and measuring the firm's activity. At the same time, the budget expresses in financial terms the firm's strategies and tactics, and it provides links to the measurement of performance and the compensation system. Without clear, unambiguous inputs from the company's planners, the budget process will invariably go awry. The planning and budgeting processes must be tailored to the firm and reflect the level of planning and the time period involved. Strategic plans represent the highest level of planning and are developed by upper management using a top-down approach. They are designed to implement the firm's goals and objectives over the long-term. Tactical plans are prepared along with the strategic plans and specify the tools and techniques employed in accomplishing the strategic objectives. Tactical plans are prepared using a bottom-up approach and have a shorter planning horizon. They are more detailed than the strategic budgets and are often prepared at the department or activity level. The strategic plan is for the company as a whole but the tactical plan describes how the various departments and functions expect to accomplish the strategic goals and objectives.

Ideally, then, budgets flow naturally from a well-coordinated budgeting process. Your firm should develop strategic and tactical plans that are integrated with the budgeting process. For each plan there should be a corresponding budget and information should flow freely between them. Done wrong, your company will simply spin its wheels and waste everybody's time on a budget that doesn't help. Done right, the budget process may still be difficult and drawn out. But it will be worth it.

Budgeting is a

black art practiced

by bureaucrat

magicians.

David Muchow, Chicago Sun Times

KEY 2

Preparing the operating budget

Planning is conducted both top-down and bottom-up. Strategic plans are developed by upper management and passed down to lower levels for implementation. The implementation or tactical plans are presented in the form of a budget. These individual budgets are consolidated and presented in the master budget.

The master budget is not a single budget but rather a portfolio of budgets. The master budget is separated into operating budgets and financial budgets. The operating budget consists of the sales budget, production budget, direct material budget, direct labor budget and a factory overhead budget.

Preparing the sales budget is the first step in generating the master budget. The sales budget should forecast sales over the relevant planning horizon. The sales forecast is prepared first because sales drive most of the other budget items. Three steps are involved in the sales forecast.

First, units sold are estimated for the budget period. Second, the sales price per unit is estimated. Third, sales revenue is estimated as the product of units sold and price per unit. A fourth step is included if sales are broken down into shorter time frames such as quarters.

Units sold and the sales price are estimated separately because they are not independent of each other. For most products the higher the price the lower the number of units sold. Historical firm-specific data, industry data and theoretical supply and demand relationships are used to estimate the best sales price. The following is an example of a simple sales budget.

	Year 1	Year 2	Year 3	Year 4
Expected sales in units	12,000	15,000	18,000	25,000
Unit sales price	$22.00	$24.50	$24.50	$27.00
Total sales	$264,000	$367,500	$441,000	$675,000

Once the sales budget is prepared the next step is to prepare the production budget. Production budgets display output by units of product manufactured or purchased. Operation managers or production supervisors use the sales budget to determine production and inventory requirements. Because manufacturing output and unit sales are not perfectly coordinated the production budget must include adjustments to allow for overproducing or underproducing. This adjustment is reflected in the inventory budget, which feeds back to the production budget. The following production budget is based on the sales budget example presented above.

	Year 1	Year 2	Year 3	Year 4
Expected sales in units	12,000	15,000	18,000	25,000
Beginning inventory	1,750	2,750	750	2,750
Production in units	13,000	13,000	20,000	25,000
Ending inventory	2,750	750	2,750	2,750

The optimal or most cost effective production run will vary depending upon the type of product, type of machinery, set up time and costs. In this model, the production run and ending inventory are managed jointly. Undue focus on inventory management can significantly increase production costs.

The direct materials budget uses the production budget to estimate the amount of direct materials needed and the associated cost. The following simplified direct materials budget is based on the production budget example presented above.

	Year 1	Year 2	Year 3	Year 4
Production in units	13,000	13,000	20,000	25,000
Amount of material needed per unit of production	2.5	2.5	2.8	2.8
Amount of material needed	32,500	32,500	56,000	70,000
Cost per unit of direct material	$1.00	$1.50	$2.00	$2.50
Total projected materials cost	$32,500	$48,750	$112,000	$175,000

If multiple products are being produced that compete for materials, the materials budget should be expanded to clearly disclose which products are using materials most efficiently.

Like the materials budget, the direct labor budget is designed to assign dollar costs to budgeted units of production. The direct labor budget estimates direct labor costs for each product produced. The steps involved in producing the budget are straightforward. First, direct labor hours per unit produced are estimated. Second, the dollar cost per labor hour is determined. Finally, total labor hours are multiplied by the hourly labor rate to determine total direct labor costs. The following is an example of a single product direct labor budget.

	Year 1	Year 2	Year 3	Year 4
Production in units	13,000	13,000	20,000	25,000
Hours of direct labor needed per unit of production	1.5	1.5	1.1	1.0
Total direct labor hours needed for budgeted production	19,500	19,500	22,000	25,000
Direct labor cost per hour	$10.00	$11.00	$12.50	$13.00
Total projected direct labor cost	$195,000	$214,500	$275,000	$325,000

These costs represent expected or average direct labor costs. Change in technology or economic conditions may significantly alter the need for highly trained labor and reduce labor costs.

The final component of the operating budget is the factory overhead budget. Factory overhead is comprised of all operating costs that are not directly traceable to a product. These costs include items such as indirect materials, indirect labor, management salaries and facility costs like utilities and rent or depreciation. They are not easily identified with a product and are often allocated to individual products or departments in an ad hoc basis such as floor space, number of employees or units of production.

KEY 3

Preparing the financial budget

The financial budget consists of the capital expenditure budget and the cash budget. These budgets support the operating budgets. The capital expenditure budget estimates the financing requirements needed for major asset purchases. The cash budget projects cash flows and short-term financing and investment decisions. Information from the master budget is used to produce *pro forma* financial statements, essentially the advance estimates of where the company expects to be in terms of profits, revenues and net assets at the end of the reporting period. The operating budgets provide the information needed to generate the *pro forma* income statement. The capital expenditure budget updates the balance sheet to reflect fixed asset acquisitions. The cash budget uses information generated by the operating budgets to update the cash and short-term investment account on the *pro forma* balance sheet.

The capital expenditure budget contains purchases of machinery, facilities or other long-term projects.

The items included are the projects that management has selected to create value. The very survival of the firm hinges on the projects included in the capital budget. Because of their importance and the large dollar amounts involved they are carefully analyzed. Most firms have a separate capital budgeting department to evaluate potential projects. The analysis usually consists of comparing the projected ability of the project to generate cash with its net investment. Occasionally the analysis includes a charge for using the capital. The capital charge is usually expressed in percentage terms. For example, the firm may require all capital budget expenditures to generate a rate of return in excess of a hurdle rate such as 20%. The major deficiency in the capital expenditure budget is that it is rarely used as a budget. Even though it is subjected to the most rigorous analysis, once the budget is approved subsequent performance is usually ignored. The operating and cash budgets are continuously monitored and significant deviations investigated. If the capital expenditure budget is to fulfill its role as a planning and monitoring tool its long-term nature must be recognized. Just because the project's investment is budgeted in a single period does not mean that its benefits are limited to that period. Each year, during its useful life, the project should be evaluated. Its continuing value should be compared to its salvage value. If the estimated salvage value exceeds the projected continuing value, the project should be terminated and the proceeds included in the budget.

The cash budget estimates cash receipts and disbursements over the planning period. It is used to monitor liquidity and aid in borrowing or investment decisions. The cash budget is broken into six sections. The first is the initial cash balance. The second presents estimated cash receipts.

Cash receipts represent money received from cash sales, collection of accounts receivable and other cash inflows like interest or dividends. This is obtained from the sales budget. The third section is cash disbursements. Cash disbursements include disbursements for cash purchases, wages, taxes, dividends, interest and principal payments and payments on account. This is obtained from the materials, direct labor and factory overhead budgets. The fourth section is the cash balance before any investments or additional financing. The fifth section shows the desired final cash position for that period. This is based on management's selected level of liquidity. The sixth section shows any short-term financing or investments.

Cash budgets often consolidate the cash collections and disbursements of several departments or branches into a few accounts. That helps reduce the uncertainty associated with constantly fluctuating cash balances. The lower the uncertainty in the cash balance, the lower the chance of having insufficient money on hand and the lower the minimum level of liquidity that must be maintained, leaving more money available for investment. Commercial demand deposits at banks do not earn interest. So, as much cash as possible should be held in short-term low risk securities like Treasury bills and highly rated commercial paper.

KEY 4

Use budgets to plan and control. Use pro forma financial statements to measure and monitor value creation

Budgets are designed primarily to help managers implement their plans. They also provide a means to control and monitor performance. This means that managers are able to detect situations where actual results deviate from the budget and can take corrective action. This definition of performance is very different from that used by financial analysts. Both internal and external financial analysts are more concerned with monitoring and measuring earnings and value creation rather than compliance with a budget. The *pro forma* financial statements are the documents used to monitor and measure financial performance and value creation. Value creation is also called economic profit. Economic profit is lower than accounting profit by a charge for the operating assets employed.

The *pro forma* income statement is prepared using data provided by the master budget. Start with the sales forecast from the sales budget. Variable operating costs are estimated using the "percentage of sales" method. Percentage of sales is a simple approach that estimates operating costs that are a constant percentage of sales. A common method used to determine the percentage is to calculate the ratio of the historical change in sales to the change in operating costs. Industry averages or more sophisticated firm-specific projections, such as regression analysis, can also be used. These methods are discussed in a later key. Fixed operating costs are estimated using data from the projected balance sheet and the factory overhead budget. Depreciation is usually the largest fixed cost. The following is an example of a *pro forma* income statement.

	Year 1	Year 2
Estimated sales from the sales budget	$264,000	$367,500
Estimated variable operating expenses		
(% of projected sales, 55% and 52%)	147,500	191,100
Estimated fixed operating expenses		
depreciation (from *pro forma* balance sheet)	35,000	42,000
Other fixed operating expenses	15,750	18,500
Earnings before interest and taxes (EBIT)	$65,750	$115,900
Estimated interest expense (from the cash budget)	1,100	1,100
Estimated non-operating revenue	500	750
Estimated other non-operating expenses	1,750	3,200
Earnings before taxes (EBT)	$63,400	$112,350
Estimated taxes (28%)	13,948	24,717
Earnings after taxes (EAT) or net income	$49,452	$87,633
Number of shares of common stock outstanding	100,000	100,000
Estimated earnings per share (EPS)	$0.49	$0.88

The above example is typical. It separates revenue and expenses into their operating and non-operating components but lumps taxes into one item. Another accounting format often used is the single-step presentation. Here all revenue items are grouped together regardless of whether they are operating or non-operating. Likewise, all expenses are grouped together.

This approach clearly shows the impact of revenues and expenses but doesn't allow easy measurement of the profits generated by operations. Both approaches focus on measuring accounting profits, but they are not designed to help measure the estimated value created or destroyed if the current plans and budgets are implemented. In order to measure the estimated value creation or destruction, a third approach developed by firms such as Stern Stewart must be used.

The Stern Stewart model focuses on Net Operating Profit after Taxes (NOPAT). This is similar to the EBIT model shown in the previous table less operating taxes (EBIT times the tax rate). NOPAT is used to calculate economic value added (EVA). The following is an example of a NOPAT calculation.

	Year 1	Year 2
EBIT	$67,750	$115,900
Accounting adjustment	21,650	38,300
Adjusted net operating profit	$46,100	$77,600
Other income	500	750
Net operating profit before taxes	$46,600	$78,350
Cash operating taxes	10,252	17,237
NOPAT	$36,348	$61,113

The accounting adjustments are designed to remove distortions in operating profits caused by Generally Accepted Accounting Principles (GAAP). The adjustments vary depending on the particular firm. A typical adjustment would be the implied interest expense on non-capitalized leases. Another adjustment would be to remove any amortization of goodwill and recognize it as an asset. Goodwill occurs when a firm purchases another firm for more than the fair market value of the acquired firm's tangible assets. The cash operating tax calculation is also unique to the Stern Stewart approach. Cash operating taxes adjust the income statement tax provision to remove the impact of deferred taxes and any tax reduction generated by interest expenses.

The NOPAT is considered to be a better measure of the firm's true operating profits and is used as an estimate of the cash return generated by the firm's operations. It is net of depreciation in order to reflect the need to retain a certain amount of cash to replace machinery and equipment as it wears out. Economic profits are calculated by reducing NOPAT by a capital use charge. For example, assume that the firm used $120,000 of assets in year 1 and $300,000 in year 2 to produce the NOPAT shown above. Also assume that the firm requires a 15% return on its invested assets.

	Year 1	Year 2
NOPAT	$36,348	$61,113
Capital Charge:		
($120,000 × 15%)	18,000	
($300,000 × 15%)		45,000
Economic profit	$18,348	$16,113

Note that accounting profits were higher in year 2 but economic profits were higher in year 1. This is because the firm used fewer resources to produce year 1 profits.

KEY 5

The budget must consider cost behavior

Information concerning the variability of cost with output and other decision variables is essential to preparing the budget. These factors must be separated and their impact measured. The most common method is to classify them into three general categories: fixed, variable and semi-variable.

Fixed costs do not vary with changes in sales. For example, depreciation is a fixed cost. It is a function of the level of depreciated fixed assets on the *pro forma* balance sheet and the depreciation method. Straight line depreciation is the most common depreciation method used. Installed cost, net of estimated salvage value, is allocated evenly over the asset's expected life. Tax authorities allow firms to use a different method for book and tax depreciation. Therefore, tax expense is often calculated using an accelerated depreciation method. Different depreciation methods are used so that book income will be maximized and the tax bill minimized. All depreciation methods are criticized for not reflecting the actual reduction in asset value, i.e. economic depreciation. While depreciation is a major fixed cost, it is usually not the firm's only fixed charge. Property taxes, rent, insurance and amortization of intangible assets are also fixed costs.

Variable costs move directly with changes in sales. It is important that the proper cost pattern is identified and reflected in the relevant budget and *pro forma* income statement. Several methods are used to identify variable cost patterns. The high-low method is the simplest. Using direct labor as an example, a representative time period such as one month is selected. High and low unit sales and high and low direct labor hours for the month are identified. The difference in direct labor hours is divided by the difference in units sold. The resulting ratio is the percentage change in direct labor hours for each unit sold. The following is an example of the high-low method.

	High	Low	Difference
Units sold	15,000	4,500	10,500
Direct labor hours used	1,875	150	1,725

Variable rate = 1,725/10,500 = 0.1643 or 16.43%

According to the above example each unit sold requires 0.1643 hours of direct labor. Therefore, if 5,000 units are sold approximately 821 hours of direct labor is needed. Direct labor costs are estimated by multiplying the direct labor hours by the hourly rate. If the hourly rate is $12 per hour, direct labor costs are estimated at $9,852.

Semi-variable costs vary with sales but they also have a fixed component. Utilities represent a semi-variable cost. Electricity and heating or cooling costs vary with the level of activity, but as long as the plant remains open there is a minimum cost. The high-low method can be used to calculate semi-variable costs but there is a much better tool. Most firms have access to software such as Lotus, Quattro or Excel. These packages include a function referred to as regression analysis. Regression is much more accurate than the high-low method and is very easy to use. The following example uses one week of utility costs to estimate the fixed and variable portions.

	Mon	Tue	Wed	Thur	Fri
Utility costs	$1,250	$2,400	$1,710	$1,900	$850
Unit sales	5,600	7,500	6,600	7,200	300

The regression results from Excel identify the following relationship.

$$\text{Utility costs} = 677.05 + 0.1737 \text{ (unit sales)}$$
$$R \text{ square} = 0.74$$

According to these results utility costs have a fixed component of $677.05 per day. In addition to the fixed portion, utility costs also vary with sales. Each unit of sales is associated with about $0.1737 in utility costs. At 4,000 sales units utility costs are estimated to be:

$$\$677.05 + 0.1737(4,000) = \$1,371.85$$

The R square is used to provide a level of confidence in the regression estimates. If the R square is close to one then the estimate can be used. If the R square is close to zero there is no relationship between sales and utility costs. In the example, the R square is 0.74 which is close enough to confidently use the results.

Regression analysis is a very useful tool in estimating costs. However, it still requires the analyst to check the results against reality. Remember "Garbage in, garbage out" applies to all statistical tools. Regression analysis is a tool—not a cure-all.

KEY 6

Managers must be flexible. So must their budgets

Budgets are management tools. They help plan the firm's future actions in accordance with the goals and objectives. But economic and market conditions change. If the firm is going to properly adjust to these changing conditions the budgets must be flexible. Many firms do not want to devote the additional time and effort involved in developing flexible budgets. Typically an unchanging world is assumed and revenue, costs and cash flows are estimated for a single level of sales or production activity. This can be a big mistake.

When sales vary from the forecast actual results will not agree with projections and performance reports will be distorted. Monitoring performance is a major function of the budget and it will not be effective unless the budgets are modified to allow for a range of sales level. Management must be able to adjust the budget to reflect the actual sales level. The flexible budget accomplishes this by generating a series of budgets with different sales forecasts.

A flexible budget is developed in two steps. First, the range of sales activity must be identified. For example the firm might decide that during the next year sales might be ten, twenty or thirty thousand units. The second step is to identify fixed and variable costs. Variable costs are the ones that vary proportionately or "flex" with changes in sales volume.

The example below shows how to adjust the operating profit forecast for three levels of sales activity, but more are easily possible. It could also be modified to consider potential price changes due to competition or other factors.

Units sold	10,000	20,000	30,000
Price per unit	$10	$10	$10
Sales	$100,000	$200,000	$300,000
Variable costs			
Direct labor @ $1.50	$15,000	$30,000	$ 45,000
Direct material @ $4.00	40,000	80,000	120,000
Overhead @ $2.50	25,000	50,000	75,000
Total variable costs $8.00	$80,000	$160,000	$240,000
Contribution margin $2.00	$20,000	$40,000	$60,000
Fixed costs			
Depreciation	7,500	7,500	7,500
Overhead	16,250	16,250	16,250
Total fixed costs	$23,750	$23,750	$23,750
Operating profit (loss)	($3,750)	$16,250	$36,250

Incorporating flexibility into the budget process makes the budget performance reports more useful because both budget and actual results are based on the same level of activity. The following examples use the data presented above to compare fixed and flexible budget performance reports.

FIXED BUDGET PERFORMANCE REPORT

	Budget	Actual	Difference
Units sold	20,000	10,000	(10,000)
Sales @ $10/unit	$200,000	$130,000	($70,000)
Variable costs			
Direct labor	$30,000	$24,000	$6,000
Direct material	80,000	47,000	33,000
Overhead	50,000	20,000	30,000
Total variable costs	$160,000	$91,000	($69,000)
Contribution margin	$40,000	$39,000	($1,000)
Fixed costs			
Depreciation	7,500	7,500	0
Overhead	16,250	17,000	(750)
Total fixed costs	$23,750	$24,500	($750)
Operating profit (loss)	$16,250	$14,500	($1,750)

According to the fixed budget performance report the firm's operating profits were $1,750 lower than projected. Based on the performance report revenues were too low and costs were high. But considering that sales were ten thousand units lower than expected does the performance report accurately reflect operating results? The flexible budget performance report presented below shows a different picture.

FLEXIBLE BUDGET PERFORMANCE REPORT			
	Budget	**Actual**	**Difference**
Units sold	10,000	10,000	(10,000)
Sales @ $10/unit	$100,000	$130,000	$30,000
Variable costs			
Direct labor	$15,000	$24,000	($9,000)
Direct material	40,000	47,000	($7,000)
Overhead	25,000	20,000	5,000
Total variable costs	$80,000	$91,000	($11,000)
Contribution margin	$20,000	$39,000	$19,000
Fixed costs			
Depreciation	7,500	7,500	0
Overhead	16,250	17,000	(750)
Total fixed costs	$23,750	$24,500	($750)
Operating profit (loss)	($3,750)	$14,500	$18,250

The flexible budget performance report evaluates performance based on the same level of unit sales. According to the flexible budget performance report the firm outperformed expectations by almost $20,000. Instead of an operating loss of $3,750 the firm generated profits of $18,250. This is a much more realistic evaluation of cost and revenue performance than the fixed budget performance report.

KEY 7

The budget must consider revenue behavior

Revenue is the primary variable used to develop the *pro forma* income statement, cash budget, accounting profits, and changes in firm value. Because of its importance, the analyst must understand how revenue behaves over time and under various economic conditions. The analysis needs to be done in order to determine both the expected level of revenue and the degree of uncertainty.

Revenue behavior depends on the firm's operating assets. If the firm invests in low risk assets such as Treasury bills, the revenue level will be known with certainty. On the other hand, if the firm invests in risky assets such as exploratory oil wells the revenue level will be very uncertain. This uncertainty is called business risk. The impact of business risk on operating profits is magnified by the use of fixed operating assets. If revenues are budgeted to increase, man-ager's can use fixed operating costs to "lever up" the firm and improve operating profits. Similarly, if revenues are budgeted to decrease, fixed operating costs can be decreased.

If managers are to effectively use fixed operating costs to improve profit performance, they must be able to measure business risk. The most popular method used to measure business risk is the degree of operating leverage (DOL). This is the ratio of the percent change in operating profits for a one percent change in revenue. The following example uses DOL to measure business risk.

	Revenue	Operating Profits (EBIT)
Current level	$1,200,000	$540,000
Budgeted level	$2,500,000	$725,000

$$DOL = [(725 - 540)/540]/$$
$$[(2,500 - 1,200)/1,200] = 0.316 \text{ or } 31.6\%$$

The DOL of 31.6% means that for every one percent move in revenue up or down from the current level of $1.2 million, operating profits will move up or down 31.6% from their current level of $540,000. The DOL measure is sensitive to the base level and must be recalculated for different base levels.

Another method used to measured business risk is the operating break-even point (OBP). The OBP is the level of sales that generated zero operating profits. In order to determine the OBP, the analyst must first measure the firm's contribution margin (CM). The CM is sales minus variable operating costs and measures the amount of funds available to cover fixed operating costs. The following example shows how to calculate the OBP.

Units	Revenue	Variable Operating Costs	Fixed Operating Costs (FOC)
3,500	$6,580,000	$4,277,000	$1,880,000

Balancing the budget is like going to heaven. Everybody wants to do it, but nobody wants to do what you have to do to get there.

Phil Gramm

$$CM = \$6,580,000 - \$4,277.000 = \$2,303,000$$

$$\text{Unit } CM = \$2,303,000/3,500 = \$658$$

$$CM \text{ ratio} = \$2,303,000/\$6,580,000 = .35 \text{ or } 35\%$$

$$OBP \text{ (units)} = FOC/\text{Unit } CM = \$1,880,000/\$658$$
$$= 2,857 \text{ units}$$

$$OBP \text{ (dollars)} = FOC/CM \text{ ratio} = \$1,880,000/.35$$
$$= \$5,371,429$$

The results in the example show that if the firm sells 2,957 units generating revenue of $5,371,429 it will have a zero net operating profit (EBIT). If profits and costs are plotted on a graph, the OBP is the point where the profit line intersects the cost line.

The operating break-even chart clearly shows how revenues and profits vary with changes in sales volume. The steeper the line, the more sensitive revenue and profits are to changes in unit sales.

The break-even analysis approach shown previously assumes that all fixed costs are covered out of income. In other words, a difference between the quantity of units produced and the quantity sold has no effect on the break-even quantity or on the firm's profits. Any quantity of products put into or taken out of inventory are valued at variable costs only. This is not the approach used to prepare the production budget and *pro forma* financial statements. Accounting standards require that fixed costs are also allocated to items in inventory and it is possible to extend the break-even model to allocate fixed costs to inventory. The operating break-even point and break-even chart provide information about the potential profitability of different courses of action. Used together these techniques determine the alternative providing the optimal expected profit for a given level of operating risk.

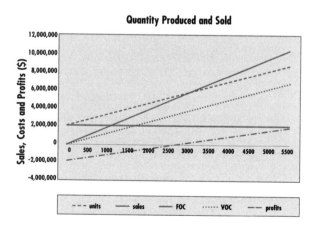

Quantity Produced and Sold

KEY 8

Profits are good. Liquidity is essential for survival

Traditionally most budgets focused on profits. The greater the accounting profits, it was assumed, the healthier and wealthier the firm and its owners. During the last 20 years the focus has shifted from accounting profits to cash flow. It is no longer sufficient to understand revenue and cost behavior. Cash flow behavior must also be analyzed.

Cash flows are important to the firm for two reasons. First, projected cash flows are the foundation for capital budgeting decisions and are a fundamental part of the firm's long-term success. Second, cash flows are used to manage short-term liquidity. Until about two decades ago liquidity management focused on the balance sheet and used some sort of measure to determine if the firm had sufficient current assets to cover short-term cash needs. Short-term assets were defined as those assets expected to be converted into cash within one year and short-term cash needs were defined as those liabilities requiring cash payment within one year. Current assets include cash, marketable securities, accounts receivable, inventory, and prepaid items such as insurance. Current liabilities include accounts payable, accrued wages, short-term notes payable, dividends payable, and the currently maturing portion of long term debt. The most popular measures of balance sheet liquidity are the current ratio and acid or quick ratio. The current ratio is the ratio of current assets to current liabilities. A rule of thumb is that the current ratio should not be less than two.

The balance sheet focus turned out to be a very poor measure of liquidity and provided misleading impressions of the health of the firm. The Comprehensive Liquidity Index (CLI) attempted to improve liquidity measurement by adjusting the current ratio to include a turnover factor. Accounts receivable, inventory, accounts payable, and accrued expenses are adjusted by the following turnover factor:

$$CLI = [\text{Accounts Receivable}] \times [1 - (1/ARTO)]$$
$$\text{where } ARTO = \text{Net Credit Sales/Accounts Receivable}$$

The first major attempt to improve liquidity management involved including the income statement, which provides the cash manager with the operating cash flow pattern. If the cash manager can accurately match operating cash inflows with cash outflows, then the need for balance sheet liquidity is reduced and more funds are available for more profitable investment. The cash conversion cycle (CCC) is used to measure liquidity that includes operating cash flows. The CCC is calculated as follows.

$$CCC = [(\text{Inventory} \times 365)/\text{Cost of goods}] +$$
$$[(\text{Accounts receivable} \times 365)/\text{Net sales}] -$$
$$[\text{Accounts Payable} \times 365)/\text{Purchases}]$$

The longer the CCC, the less liquid the firm. The CCC is an improvement because it adopts an approach based on the going concern rather than simply a snapshot of a single point in time. But it is still an incomplete measure of liquidity. It also does not incorporate risk.

In 1984 a new measure, Lambda, was introduced. Lambda is calculated as follows:

$$\text{Lambda} = (\text{Liquid resources} + \text{Expected cash flow})/\text{Uncertainty of cash flow}$$

Liquid resources include cash, marketable securities, and unused credit lines. Expected cash flow includes any expected or planned financing and investment as well as the net operating cash flows for the time period of the analysis. Risk or uncertainty is measured by the standard deviation of the cash flows. A major benefit of Lambda is that it can be used to estimate the probability that the liquidity position might be insufficient to prevent insolvency. For example, a Lambda of 1.65 means that there is about a 5% chance that the firm will be insolvent during the estimation horizon while a Lambda of 3 signals a 0.10% chance of insolvency.

The operating budgets project the firm's growth rate in sales and profits over the planning horizon. The capital expenditure budget allocates funds to projects projected to create value and ensure the firm's long-term survival. The focus of the cash budget and liquidity management is short-term survival. Many profitable firms enjoying a rapid rate of sales growth failed because of poor liquidity management.

KEY 9

Determining the optimal cash balance

Once the firm determines the level of liquidity needed to ensure short-term solvency it should decide on the amount that should be cash. Bank regulations in the United States prohibit paying interest on commercial checking accounts. So firms invest any excess funds in short-term interest bearing assets. How does the firm decide what constitutes excess cash? Three models are commonly used to answer this question.

The Baumol model assumes that cash flows are known with absolute certainty. It also assumes that cash inflows occur at a discrete point but cash outflows are continuous. Based on these assumptions the model determines the amount and timing of investments and disinvestments. The optimal amount of securities sold at each interval is:

$$C = \sqrt{2bT/i}$$

C is the optimal amount of securities sold.

b is the fixed transaction charge, such as commissions.

T is the known cash inflow.

i is the rate of interest the securities earn per period.

The following is an example of the Baumol model. Assume that the firm receives $1,000,000 at the beginning of each month and disburses the entire amount in a continuous stream of cash flow payments. The firm can invest in short-term securities that pay 12% per year. There is a fixed cost of $25.00 per transaction. The optimal amount of each transaction is:

$$C = \sqrt{\frac{2(\$25)(\$1,000,000)}{.12/12}} = \$70,711$$

The firm should invest $929,289 at the beginning of each month and withdraw $70,711 approximately every 2 days.

Baumol's model works well as long as the firm is steadily using up its cash inventory. But this is usually not the case. Miller and Orr developed an alternative model based on the assumption that cash flow patterns are uncertain. In other words, management has no ability to predict or accurately budget cash flows. The cash budget cannot be used for planning or control since the cash flow projection for any period is completely unknown. Using this scenario Miller and Orr developed the following cash management model.

$$z = 3[(3bs^2)/(4i)]^{1/3}$$
$$h = r + z$$

z is the spread between the upper and lower cash balance limits.

h is an upper limit that cash balances are not allowed to exceed.

r is a lower limit that cash balances are not allowed to fall below. Management sets this at whatever level it decides is appropriate.

s is the standard deviation of cash flows.

i is the rate of return earned by the short-term investment portfolio.

b is the fixed transaction cost

The following is an example of how the Miller and Orr model is used. Assume that management sets a lower cash balance limit of $15,000, the standard deviation of cash flows is $1,000 per day, the annual rate of return on the short-term investment portfolio is 10% and each purchase or sale of securities costs $25.

$$z = 3[(3(\$25)(\$1,000)^2)/(4(.027\%))]^{1/3} = \$12,270$$

Management set the lower limit at $15,000. The upper limit is $r \times z$ or $15,000 + 12,270 = \$27,270$. The return point is $r + z/3$ or $19,090. Based on these numbers if the cash balance rises to $27,270, invest $27,270 − $19,090 in marketable securities. If the cash balance falls to $15,000, sell $4,090 or marketable securities and replenish cash.

Stone developed a cash management model that lies between the Baumol and Miller and Orr models. The Stone model assumes that management has some cash forecasting ability and represents the cash flows as consisting of a portion that can be forecast and a portion that is random. The model contains two sets of control limits. Cash balances are allowed to fluctuate within the inner control limits, but if the outer control limits are touched management takes action.

When the outer control limits are touched, management uses its cash flow forecast for the next *k* days. If the projected cash balance is within the inner control limits no further action is taken. If the projected cash balance is outside the inner control limits, securities are purchased or sold to bring the projected cash balance back to the target balance or return point. The following is an example of the Stone model.

Assume that management has established outer limits of $100,000 and $10,000 and inner limits of $90,000 and $20,000. Further assume that the targeted cash balance is $50,000 and the firm starts with a cash balance of $60,000. For the first ten days the cash balance is within the outer control limit so no action is taken. On day ten the cash balance is $110,000, which exceeds the upper control limit. This is a signal for the manager to check the cash forecast for the next *k* days. Management decides on the number of days to look ahead; assume that it is three days. From the cash forecast it appears that the cash balance on day thirteen will be $95,000. This is outside the inner control limit so management will invest $45,000 in marketable securities to bring the forecasted cash balance down to the $50,000 target level on day thirteen.

KEY 10

Part of planning and budgeting is setting standards

The budgeting process usually involves collecting historical revenue and cost data that can be used to determine the profits that result from production. Historical data can provide valuable insights, but it can be misleading since it represents what happened, not necessarily what should have happened. For example, assume that the firm is using outdated equipment and production is very inefficient. Ideally, the firm would recognize the problem and collect data permitting management to develop a plan based on a more efficient use of resources.

Budgets should not be based on historical results if management determines that operations were inefficient. Plans and budgets should be based on what we want to happen. Standard costs are developed to allow budgets to be based on efficient operations and should be used to inform employees of what costs should be. Since standard costs are predetermined estimates of what costs should be—assuming efficient operations—

they can be used as part of the firm's compensation system. For example, a bonus plan can be established to reward employees that complete their work within the standard time allowed.

Standard costs are easy to calculate once the necessary information is provided. Gathering the information needed to measure a standard cost, however, can be time consuming and expensive. Once the data is gathered, the standard cost is made up of a unit price and level of input. For example, if it was determined that eight hours of direct labor and an hourly rate of $10 per hour were required to produce one unit of a product the standard direct labor cost would be $80. Other examples of standards are sales quotas and standard volume.

Standard costs can vary depending on how tough management wants to be. Ideal standard costs are based on the assumption that the operation will be performed at the maximum level of efficiency. That doesn't happen very often, so using them can lead to employee dissatisfaction. Most firms prefer to use attainable standard costs. These are based on a "reasonable" level of effort and efficiency.

Standard costs allow firms to plan and budget operations based on a given level of efficiency and assign responsibility for any deviation or variance from the plan. Variances can arise for a variety of reasons: entry of new competitors, improved technology, labor negotiations, unexpected increase in fuel costs, etc. Variance analysis is used to identify budget variances. Once a variance is identified it is classified as significant or insignificant, controllable, partly controllable, or uncontrollable. All significant variances should be examined but action is only taken on significant controllable or partly controllable variances.

Managers often overlook the planning variance. The planning variance occurs when supply and demand for the firm's product is different than expected. An example of a planning variance is an unexpected price war. As a result, sales are lower than expected. This is a planning error but since it shows up as a sales variance management might be tempted to interpret it as poor performance. Don't. Planning variances that are not controllable should not be used to monitor and control the marketing and sales staff.

A true sales variance involves sales generating activities that are controllable by the sales staff. The following is an example of a sales variance report.

Total Sales Variance	
Budgeted sales for 10,000 units @ $4.50 per unit	$45,000
Actual sales of 11,000 units @ $3.00 per unit	$33,000
Unfavorable sales variance	$12,000
Price Variance	
Unfavorable price variance due to sales of	
11,000 units at $3.00 instead of $4.50	$16,500
Quantity Variance	
Favorable variance due to sales of	
11,000 units instead of 10,000 at $4.50	$4,500

The sales price variance shows that the product was being sold for less than budgeted. The quantity variance shows that more units were sold than budgeted. The two variances had the opposite effect on sales revenue but overall the sales department performed below expectations. Variance analysis should be conducted to determine why the deviations occurred. The price variance could have been caused by a new sales department manager attempting to increase total sales with a price reduction.

Standard cost variances occur when actual costs differ from predetermined standard costs. The following is an example of a direct labor variance report.

Total Direct Labor Variance

Standard hours × standard rate: 10,000 × $6.50	$65,000
Actual hours × actual rate: 8,000 × $9.00	72,000
Unfavorable total labor variance	$7,000

Direct Labor Rate Variance

Actual hours × (Actual rate − Standard rate): 8,000 × $2.50	$20,000
This is an unfavorable labor rate variance	

Direct Labor Efficiency Variance

Standard rate × (Actual hours − Standard hours): $6.50 × 2,000	$13,000
This is a favorable labor efficiency variance	

The direct labor variance report shows that the department was more efficient than planned but the employees received higher wages. The department manager may have been notified that the employees were planning to strike. In order to complete the project the manager paid bonuses if it was completed before the strike.

KEY 11

Selecting and using the best cost allocation methods

enerally accepted accounting principles require absorption costing to be used for external reporting purposes. Absorption costing allocates certain production costs between cost of goods sold and inventory. For example, if the firm produced 1,000 units and sold 800, 80% of the production costs would be allocated to cost of goods sold and 20% allocated to ending inventory. But for internal reports, management often needs information that will help measure the impact of changes in sales volume on the costs and profits. This is impossible with absorption costing since it makes no clear-cut distinction between fixed and variable costs.

Variable costing is an alternative cost accounting method that is frequently used for internal reporting. Variable costing allocates production costs entirely to the cost of goods sold. In the above example, variable costing would allocate 80% of variable production costs and 100% of fixed production costs to costs of goods sold. The

200 units added to inventory would be valued at 20% of the variable production costs. Variable costing provides the information needed for break-even analysis. The separation of fixed and variable costs also helps management evaluate new product and allocate resources.

Neither absorption nor variable costing allows management to properly manage products and costs. A new cost accounting method called activity based costing (ABC) attempts to improve product costing; it is based on the idea that cost objects consume activities, activities consume resources, and the consumption of resources drives costs. Understanding this relationship is critical to successfully managing overhead. The following example shows how an ABC system works.

Assume that Acme Manufacturing Inc. makes two products, product A and product B. Each product incurs direct labor, direct materials and overhead costs.

Production Data	A	B
Production	13,000	7,500
Direct material cost per unit	$10	$12
Direct labor rate per hour	18	18
Number of direct labor hour per unit produced	4	2
Total overhead is $143,675 of which $37,575 is fixed		

Overhead per unit of production depends on the cost accounting method used.

PRODUCT COST USING ABSORPTION COSTING
Assume that overhead is allocated to products based on the ratio of direct labor hours used.

A:	13,000 units	×	4 hours	=	52,000 hours
B:	7,500 units	×	2 hours	=	15,000 hours
Total hours				67,000 hours

Overhead allocation rate: $143,675 overhead / 67,000 hours = $2.1444/ hour.

A:	4 hour	=	$8.5776
B:	2 hour	=	$4.2889

Absorption Product Cost	A	B
Direct material	$10.00	$12.00
Direct labor	18.00	18.00
Overhead	8.58	4.29
Total	$36.58	$34.29

PRODUCT COST USING VARIABLE COSTING

As in the absorption costing example, overhead is allocated to products based on the ratio of direct labor hours used. In this example, however, only variable overhead of $106,100 is allocated to products. The $37,575 of fixed overhead is treated as a period expense.

Overhead allocation rate: $106,100 overhead / 67,000 hours = $1.5836/ hour.

A:	4 hour	=	$6.3343
B:	2 hour	=	$3.1672

Variable Product Cost	A	B
Direct material	$10.00	$12.00
Direct labor	18.00	18.00
Overhead	6.33	3.17
Total	$34.33	$33.17

PRODUCT COST USING ACTIVITY BASED COSTING

Step 1: Identify activities, activity drivers and activity costs.

Activity	Activity driver	Driver			Activity
		A	B	Total	Cost
Buying raw material	# of purchase orders	1,700	1,100	2,800	$2,375
Equipment prep	# of machine setups	75	125	200	8,000
Making the item	machine hours	17,600	8,900	26,500	85,000
Shipping	# of deliveries	28,000	18,000	46,000	48,300
Total activity cost					$143,675

Step 2: Divide total costs by total drivers to determine rate per driver.

Activity	Cost/Driver	
Buying raw material	$2,375/2,800	= $0.8482
Equipment preparation	$8,000/200	= $40.0000
Making the item	$85,000/26,500	= $3.2075
Shipping	$48,300/46,000	= $1.0500

Step 3: Multiply the rate by the number of drivers for each activity for each product to calculate the overhead dollars for each activity.

Activity	Rate	A		B	
		Number	Cost	Number	Cost
Buying raw material	$0.8482	1,700	$1,442	1,100	$933
Equipment preparation	40.0000	75	3,000	125	5,000
Making the item	3.2075	17,600	56,452	8,900	28,548
Shipping	1.0500	28,000	29,400	18,000	18,900

Step 4: Add overhead dollars to calculate total overhead dollars per product.

Activity	A	B
Buying raw material	$1,442	$933
Equipment preparation	3,000	5,000
Making the item	56,452	28,548
Shipping	29,400	18,900
Total overhead dollars	$90,294	$53,381

Step 5: Divide total overhead dollars for a product by the number of units produced to achieve the new overhead rate per unit.

A	$90,294/13,000 units	=	$6.95
B:	$53,381/7,500 units	=	$35.59

Step 6: Calculate the new product cost.

ABC Product Cost	A	B
Direct material	$10.00	$12.00
Direct labor	18.00	18.00
Overhead	6.95	35.59
Total	$34.95	$65.59

Traditional absorption based costing estimated product costs at $36.58 and $34.29. According to this method, product costs are very similar. Variable costing estimated product costs at $34.33 and $33.17. Product costs are generally lower using variable costing since fixed overhead is expensed in the current period. According to activity based costing, however, the estimated product costs are $34.95 and $65.59. Budgeted product costs are very different depending on how overhead is allocated.

If product B sells for $60 per unit it would appear to be profitable using the absorption or variable costing methods and it makes sense to continue production. But according to ABC, the product is losing money and should be discontinued.

KEY 12

Unsheath the budget ax

Just because something is in the budget doesn't mean it belongs there. But budget routine often leads to the continuation of unnecessary, inefficient or unprofitable activities. That's because, for many companies, budgets are nothing more than an allocation of funds to existing products or departments. The correct approach is to allocate funds to those activities that maximize firm value. The only way this can be achieved is by allocating funds to activities based on the value they create. Zero-based budgeting accomplishes this by treating every activity as though it is being considered for the first time.

The principle behind zero-based budgeting (ZBB) is that no activity, including products or departments, should be funded unless it produces adequate outputs. Each budget period provides an opportunity to reevaluate past decisions and ask two questions: First, are current operations efficiently accomplishing the goals established in the planning phase? Second, are there other activities or operations that would accomplish the assigned goals more efficiently? ZBB subjects every activity, new and continuing, to a type of cost-benefit analysis.

The first step in developing a zero-based budget is to group activities or projects into decision packages. Decision packages, which are a unique feature of ZBB consist of documents that includes a detailed description of different activities, functions or operations, specifies the activity's importance, and analyzes its costs and anticipated benefits. As part of the analysis the managers assembling the decision package are supposed to consider different ways to accomplish the task. If the current method is not the best then the decision package is prepared based on the preferred alternative method. The decision package identifies the current method, describes it and explains why it was not selected. It also provides an analysis of how much of the activity could be accomplished with different levels of effort. For example, the analysis might indicate that a project could provide a minimum output at 50% of the current level of operations. At any level below 50% it would be a waste of money to continue the project. This minimum level would be ranked above any additional levels of effort so that the firm doesn't reject funding the project at a minimum level of effort, terminate it and then approve an enhancement to the project. One of the most important reasons for identifying the alternative levels of effort is capital rationing. If the firm has limited funds it may be forced to support an activity at its minimum level, but if more funds become available additional levels of effort can be added.

Once the decision packages are assembled they are classified and ranked. A budget committee of top managers can do the ranking. If the package is classified as critical it may be funded before other packages producing a higher ranking. For example, a government mandated pollution control device may be funded before a profitable product line. The process of ranking the decision packages and selecting the optimal set varies among firms. Some companies submit the packages to a committee vote. Others let upper management select the final set. Whatever the ranking procedure, it is important that the decision packages for projects not selected be retained for further consideration if additional funding becomes available or the activity's priority changes.

It is very difficult to establish a set of guidelines to determine what decision packages should be developed. Different types of organizations and industries will require different decision packages. The best rule is that the decision package must be useful enough to the manager preparing the package and those evaluating it to justify the time and cost. Decision packages are expensive. Decision packages can be developed for a variety of company activities. For example, a decision package could be developed to combine the retail operations at two stores into one. The description would be to close store A and let store B service the entire sales area. The benefit from closing store A would be the savings from fewer salaries, lower facilities costs, plus the proceeds from selling it. The impact of closing store A would be lower combined sales for three months until customers became accustomed to the change. Alternatives would include keeping store A open or possibly closing a different store. Since zero-based budgeting requires managers to layer the decision package according to effort two packages might be submitted. The first package would close store A and combine operations into store B. The second package would keep both stores open.

Once the decision packages have been evaluated and ranked they are compared to a pre-established cutoff rank. Packages ranking very high should be funded. Packages barely above the cutoff rank should be funded but they would be the first to be cut if funding decreases. Packages ranking just below the cutoff point will not be currently funded but will be the first to benefit from additional funding. The final step in the zero-based budgeting process is to develop detailed budgets for the selected activities.

We are placing the burden on the broadest of shoulders. I made up my mind that in framing my budget no cupboard should be barer, no lot should be harder to bear.

Lloyd George

KEY 13

A firm's future depends, most of all, on the capital expenditure budget

S
ay the word "budget" and most people think of the annual operating budgets designed to implement short-term tactical plans. These budgets are important but they are not critical to long-term survival. Budgeting for capital expenditures, on the other hand, impacts long-term firm survival.

There is no clear conceptual difference between capital and current expenditures. Both attempt to exchange current funds for future benefits. Current expenditures are smaller, have a time horizon of less than a year and the timing of cash flows can be ignored. Capital expenditures are large, their impact extends for several years and the time value of money must be considered. Time value of money refers to the economic rule that funds should earn a reasonable rate of return while invested. Another difference between current and capital expenditures is the ability to compare costs and benefits. The short time between cost expenditure and receipt of benefits for current expenditures makes it much easier to evaluate and measure costs and benefits. Most companies subject capital expenditures to more formal and rigorous budgeting procedures than current expenditures.

The first step in developing a capital expenditure budget is to examine the firm's strategic plans and goals. For example, it may not be appropriate for a firm focusing on the retail segment of an industry to invest in manufacturing assets. The second step is to identify a set of proposed projects that are consistent with the strategic plans and are expected to increase value. This step is very important but is often overlooked.

The third step is to classify the proposed projects according to size, type of benefit, degree of dependence and type of cash flow. The evaluation of capital expenditures is costly and time consuming. By classifying the proposed projects according to the size of the initial investment the firm can identify the larger projects requiring formal analysis and the smaller projects that can be evaluated along with current expenditures. Classification by type of benefit is necessary because not all benefits are the same. For example, the benefits from a pollution control project would be evaluated differently from a new retail outlet. Another example is a company operated day care center. It would be difficult to measure the benefits from improved employee morale in terms of cash. Classifying projects by degree of dependence allows managers to separate projects into compliments and substitutes. Because of their complimentary relationship it may be necessary to consider multiple projects as a single item. In other cases the selection of one project automatically eliminates another project from consideration. Classification by their cash flow is also very important. Certain types of projects have characteristic patterns. For example, a typical investment begins with a cash outflow followed by a series of cash inflows. A typical loan starts with a cash inflow followed by a series of cash outflows. Equipment upgrades may generate only cash outflows. Classifying projects by cash flow pattern allows managers to clearly identify and evaluate alternative patterns.

The fourth step in preparing a capital expenditure budget is to measure the project's cash flows. It is obviously difficult to forecast future cash flows of a major project accurately. A simple procedure used by many firms is described below:

◆ Estimate the project's net investment. This is the initial cash outflow needed to acquire the asset. The net investment includes the invoice price and any installation, shipping, insurance and site preparation costs. In some cases such as the opening of a retail outlet, the net investment should also include any working capital investment.

◆ Prepare *pro forma* income statements for each year of the project.

◆ Convert project profits into net cash flows (NCF) using the following formula: NCF = After-tax operating profits + Tax benefit of depreciation.

◆ Recapture any working capital and asset salvage value at the end of the project.

The fifth step is to rank the proposed projects and make a selection. The ranking process is discussed in Key 14. Project selection can be done in several ways. It can be mechanical. For example, select all projects that exceed some predetermined hurdle. Selection can be subjective. Upper management could review the proposed projects and select those that executives believe are the most critical or create the most value. Finally a committee can be formed to vote on the projects.

The final step is the preparation of the capital expenditure budget. The budget contains a description of the project, justification, approved amount, expected project life, expected cash flows and selection criteria.

Money helps, though not

so much as you think

when you don't have it.

Lousie Edrich, **Insulation**

KEY 14

What should a capital budget accomplish?

A firm's capital expenditure budget is a look at its soul, its long-term plan for growth and survival. Because of its importance a major portion of the work by academics and practitioners has been devoted to improving capital budgeting techniques.

During the last 20 years capital budgeting methodology has been dominated by a set of "discounted cash flow" or "sophisticated" techniques. These are really not that sophisticated, but they do represent a significant improvement over previous methods. Their purpose is to select those capital projects that will result in the greatest wealth increase for the firm. These techniques include the internal rate of return (IRR), net present value (NPV) and the profitability index (PI).

There are several basic assumptions behind the DCF models. First, the firm wants to create value for the owners and the best way to do this is invest in projects that earn more than the cost of funds. For example, if a company raises capital at 10% it should not invest in projects earning 8%. Second, the project must also generate enough cash to pay back the original investment. The project should generate a sufficient return on investment and a return of the investment. Third, the sooner you get your money back, the better. Fourth, when forecasting cash flows, uncertainty matters. The more uncertain a cash flow, the less valuable. While these rules sound logical managers often ignore them.

The internal rate of return rule is a mathematical approach to ranking projects. It is very popular, but requires a financial calculator or computer. The first step is to determine what the firm is paying for project funds. The second step is to identify the project's cash flows. Third, the IRR is computed. Fourth, the IRR is compared to the cost of funds. If the IRR is below the cost of funds the project should be rejected. The IRR method is demonstrated in the following example.

◆ Assume that the firm must pay 11% for funds invested in the project.

◆ Expected project cash flows are as follows:

> Year 0: $1,000,000
> Year 1: $250,000
> Year 2: $500,000
> Year 3: $200,000
> Year 4: $225,000
> Year 5: $150,000

◆ Project IRR is determined using a calculator: 12%.

◆ IRR of 12% is greater than the 11%

cost of funds so the project should be included in the capital budget.

The net present value method attempts to accomplish the same objectives as the IRR method and its results are easier to interpret. The NPV rule "discounts" the cash flows at the project's cost of funds and subtracts the initial project cost. If the result is negative reject the project, otherwise it should be included in the capital budget. The NPV is also calculated using a financial calculator or computer. The NPV for the above example is $14,507. This means that project expected cash flows paid the 11% cost of funds, recovered the cost of the project and increased value by $14,507. One of the advantages of NPV over IRR is that it identifies the dollar increase in value generated for the firm by a capital expenditure.

The profitability index is used to select capital projects when the amount of funds available for investment is limited to a set amount. For example, assume that capital expenditures cannot exceed $50 million. In this case project evaluation must consider how much of the $50 million is used by each project. The capital budget should include the combination of projects that maximizes the PI and does not require more than $50 million in funding. Like the IRR and NPV, the PI requires a financial calculator or computer. The following example demonstrates how the PI approach is used. Assume that the firm is evaluating the following projects and cannot spend more than $50 million.

Project	Project Cost	PI	Rank
A	$12,500,000	1.95	3
B	25,000,000	1.80	5
C	19,000,000	2.22	2
D	43,000,000	1.90	4
E	17,000,000	2.50	1

According to the table the firm should select projects E, C and A. They have the highest PI and have a combined cost of $48.5 million. Project D is not selected because it violates the funding limit. The examples presented above either provided an estimate of the cost of project funds or, in the case of the PI, incorporated it into the model. In practice the firm will have to estimate the cost of project financing. If the cost of funds is incorrectly estimated the results produced by the DCF models are worthless. Every firm should make a serious effort to accurately measure the cost of capital.

Budget:

A mathematical

confirmation of

your suspicions.

A.A. Latmmer

KEY 15

Risk is as much a part of the capital budget as return

Think of the capital budget as the known expenditure of funds during the next budget period in anticipation of uncertain future benefits. If the discounted cash flow (DCF) techniques discussed previously are to function properly they must incorporate risk. There are two sides to the risk coin. On one face is the inherent difficulty in estimating future cash flows. On the other is the decision-maker's own attitude toward uncertainty.

Most interesting projects have uncertain future cash flows. The firm could budget $100,000 to purchase a one-year Treasury note that pays $2,000 during year one and $103,000 during year two of the budget. The Federal Government guarantees the note so the cash flows are certain and there is no risk. On the other hand, the firm could invest $100,000 in a project involving a coin flip. If the coin flip is heads the firm receives $200,000 and if the coin flip is tails the firm receives $20,000. The expected cash flow from this investment is calculated as follows:

$$(0.50) \times (\$200,000) + (0.50) \times (\$20,000) = \$110,000$$

Continue the example. Imagine that the "project" has an expected life of two years. Assume that in year 2 the firm rolls a six-sided die. If a one or two is rolled the firm receives $150,000. A three or four pays off with $120,000 and a five or six generates $90,000. Expected cash flow for year 2 is:

$$(2/6) \times (150,000) + (2/6) \times (\$120,000) + (2/6) \times (\$90,000) = \$120,000$$

The above example points out two pieces of information that are essential to risk analysis: the possible returns and the chance of getting those returns. In the example of the government note, the cash inflows were known with 100% certainty. In the second example, the cash inflows were estimated by their probability weighted average. This gives us an estimate of the uncertain cash flows but it doesn't measure their risk or uncertainty. We need a measure that allows us to compare the risk of a certain cash flow with a coin flip and roll of a die.

The data for the two year project described above is:

Year	Cash Flow	Probability	Weighted Cash Flows
0	− $100,000	1.00	− $100,000
1	$200,000	0.50	$100,000
	$20,000	0.50	$10,000
2	$150,000	0.333	$50,000
	120,000	0.333	$40,000
	90,000	0.333	$30,000

The most common measures of investment risk are the range, variance, semi-variance and standard deviation.

Year	Range
0	$100,000
1	$20,000 to $200,000
2	$90,000 to $150,000

Year 0 cash flow does not vary since it is known with certainty.

Variance: 0
Standard deviation: 0

Year 1 standard deviation is calculated as follows:

$$(\$200,000 - \$110,000)^2(0.50) +$$
$$(\$20,000 - \$110,000)^2(0.50) = \$8,100,000,000$$

$$\sqrt{\$8,100,000,000} = \$90,000$$

Year 2 standard deviation, using the same method, equals $30,000:

$$(\$150,000 - \$120,000)^2(0.333) + (\$120,000 - \$120,000)^2$$
$$(0.333) + (\$90,000 - \$120,000)^2(0.333) = \$900,000,000$$

$$\sqrt{\$900,000,000} = \$30,000$$

According to all three measures, year 1 cash flows are the most uncertain and risky. These are referred to as "absolute measures of risk." Managers are often interested in the relationship between risk and return. The coefficient of variation (CV) measures a cash flow's risk relative to its expected return. The CV is calculated by dividing the cash flow's standard deviation by its expected value.

Year	Coefficient of Variation (CV)
0	0
1	$90,000/$110,000 = 0.82
2	$30,000/$120,000 = 0.25

Once the forecast of cash flows is prepared the real challenge is to decide if a project should be accepted or rejected. This requires taking into account the level of risk decision makers are willing to tolerate. Risk aversion refers to the observed tendency for most individuals and firms to require compensation for assuming risk. Everyone has a different level of risk aversion and may rank risky projects differently. For example, assume that the firm is presented with the following projects.

Project	Rate of Return	Expected Return	Standard Deviation	Coefficient of Variation
A	15%	$100,000	$50,000	0.50
B	18%	$150,000	$100,000	0.667
C	22%	$200,000	$125,000	0.625
D	30%	$400,000	$280,000	0.70

Project A has the lowest risk and the lowest expected return while project D has the highest risk and the highest expected return. If only expected return mattered, we would select project D. If only risk matters, we would select project A. But since both are important, we cannot rank the projects until we know the decision makers' level of risk aversion. Many firms adjust for risk by classifying projects into risk classes, i.e., we could classify projects A and B into risk class I, project C into risk class II, and project D into risk class III. Hurdle rates are then established for each class depending on the firm's risk tolerance. Assume the firm sets hurdle rates of 17%, 25% and 30% for the respective risk classes. According to this ranking system projects B and D are acceptable because they meet or exceed their hurdle rates. The point to remember is that the assets included in a capital budget involve a trade-off between risk and return. When evaluating alternative projects, the central question is not "What's the rate of return?" It is: "Is the return sufficient to justify the risk?"

KEY 16

The "unsophisticated" rules are more useful than you might think

---

Discounted cash flow (DCF) techniques are theoretically superior to traditional or "unsophisticated" capital budgeting techniques, but they are a lot more complex and require access to extra data. In many cases this additional data is not readily available and must be estimated, which can lead to substantial distortions and misleading answers. If the potential for significant error is present, managers often prefer to base their analysis on less sophisticated "traditional" techniques, which are not as sensitive to such problems.

The traditional techniques are also known as rules of thumb. The two most widely used rules of thumb are accounting rate of return (ARR) and the payback period (PB). ARR is the ratio of the project's annual net annual profit to its total or average investment cost.

$$ARR = \frac{Net\ income}{Initial\ investment}$$

For example, a project is expected to earn $125,000 each year for twenty years and will require a $1 million investment over the next two years. The project's ARR is 125,000/1,000,000 or 12.5%. Management evaluates the project by comparing the ARR to a predetermined benchmark. The drawback to the ARR approach is that it relies on accounting data, does not consider all of the project's cash flows and ignores the cost of project funds.

Recently, however, a consulting firm, Stern Stewart and Company, introduced a new technique called economic value added (EVA™). EVA™ uses adjusted accounting profits and investment to determine a project's annual net present value (NPV) or internal rate of return (IRR). Except for accounting adjustments the calculation of ARR and EVA's™ version of annual IRR are very similar.

$$\text{EVA}^{™}(\text{ROR}) = \frac{\text{Net operating profit after taxes}}{\text{Initial investment}}$$

Another popular rule of thumb to use in selecting projects is the payback period (PB). A project's PB reflects the time it takes for expected cash inflows to equal the initial investment. In the example presented above it will take eight years before the expected cash flows equal the $1 million initial investment. Like the accounting rate of return, the payback method violates many of the principles advanced by the DCF users. For example, only cash flows received prior to the payback period are considered and the timing of these cash flows is ignored. Still, it is a useful measure of investment risk, in part because advancements in technology and changing lifestyles have reduced the life cycle of many products. Determining the payback period is useful in evaluating whether a product will last long enough to generate an acceptable return.

One long-cited advantage of DCF is that it allows users to adjust cash flows for risk or uncertainty. This risk adjustment reflects the uncertainty of the cash flow. For example, a cash flow that can be either $50,000 or $100,000 is riskier than a cash flow that is expected to vary between $70,000 and $80,000. But the DCF methods do not incorporate uncertainty about the duration of these cash flows. This type of uncertainty can occur when a project may be terminated prematurely. For example, a manufacturing firm may enter into a ten-year contract to provide a product to a large retail firm. The contract allows the retail firm to terminate the contract after five years in exchange for a $100,000 termination payment. In this situation the manufacturing firm may not undertake the project unless it can be sure that it will recapture its investment within five years. It is becoming increasingly common for projects to include "flexibility" options that allow one party to terminate, or in some way modify, the project's cash flows. DCF methods can be modified to incorporate certain types of flexibility but they are very complex and difficult to use. The payback period is a convenient rule of thumb that allows managers to consider these "flexibility" options.

The discounted cash flow approach dominates project evaluation these days, but the old rules of thumb are still used frequently as secondary screening devices to estimate such things as the value created in a single period and help evaluate flexibility options. In the future better data sources and more advanced software may eliminate the need for the traditional methods, but they currently serve a useful function.

KEY 17

You can't budget without forecasts

The future cannot be predicted with any certainty but companies have no choice but to live in it. So they develop both long-term and short-term plans aimed at maximizing the wealth of their owners. These plans specify the outputs that must be generated to accomplish the firm's mission and goals. Budgets formally present the inputs needed to produce the planned output. The budgets are only as useful as the plans on which they are based. The plans, in turn, are only as useful as the decisions that they incorporate. Finally the decisions are only as good as their underlying assumptions and forecasts. Managers have long recognized that uncertainty is part of predicting the future. But it is only in the last few decades that forecasting has assumed a critical role in the budgeting process. Advancements in computers and forecasting software have contributed to the increased use of forecasts, but they are not the primary reason.

The major motive behind improved forecasting techniques is that the future is becoming even

We might come closer to balancing the budget if all of us lived closer to the commandments and the golden rule.

Ronald Reagan

more uncertain. The business environment is becoming increasingly competitive, new foreign markets are opening, deregulation has made economic conditions less predictable and product life cycles are decreasing. Stable business conditions appear to be a thing of the past. The more managers can reduce this uncertainty, the better they can anticipate changes and the better their decision-making. The purpose of forecasting is to reduce the riskiness of decision making.

Forecasting methods are classified according to several criteria: the time horizon; whether they are qualitative and quantitative; and the level of detail, either macro or micro. The appropriate forecasting method will usually differ depending on the particular need. A forecasting technique should never be selected simply because it is complex or sophisticated. If management cannot use the output to improve its decision-making, the technique is worthless.

Long-term forecasts differ from short-term forecasts in several ways. First, long-term forecasts usually require less detail. Second, long-term forecasts are subject to a greater chance that an unexpected event will occur that significantly changes the business environment. This type of uncertainty makes it difficult to base forecasts on historical data. It may be better to use judgment-based forecasts of specialists or individuals within the firm. Judgmental or qualitative forecasts can be generated in several ways. It may represent the consensus opinion of a group of experts. It may be the result of a consumer focus group study. It may also be the result of a survey of opinions of company executives or members of the sales staff.

Quantitative forecast methods are classified into two types. The first uses historical data in an attempt to predict the future. The second assumes a causal relationship between two items such as sales volume and sales revenue. Once the primary variable, sales volume, is estimated the value of the related variable is forecast using the assumed relationship. Because of their mathematical framework quantitative forecasts are often considered superior to the qualitative methods. This isn't true. Quantitative models assume a stable environment and they do not work well in changing or unstable conditions. For example, assume that the marketing manager is aware of certain factors that are going to cause sales revenue to deviate from the level predicted by past trends. In this case a qualitative forecast may be more accurate. It is also possible to combine both methods and modify the quantitative forecast to account for the expected deviations in sales. Managers must be able to evaluate a situation, determine what is needed and select the appropriate forecasting method. For budgeting purposes what is important is that the managers trust the forecasts—not their mathematical elegance.

Regardless of the method used, the forecasting process should proceed as follows: First, and most importantly, the problem should be clearly identified and evaluated. Managers decide what they want to forecast and why. They also need to decide in advance how accurate the forecast should be and the resources they are willing to commit to preparing it. Second, the forecast horizon must be established. Are you forecasting next year's depreciation expense or are you trying to forecast a project's cash flows over the next twenty years? Third, select a macro-forecast or a micro-forecast and a qualitative or quantitative model. Fourth, collect data and inspect it for errors and relevance. Use the data to test and select among the alternative forecasting techniques. Only then is the forecast actually made. Finally, take a careful look at the accuracy of previous forecasts. This allows managers to modify or switch forecasting methods if necessary.

Remember that forecasts are one of the building blocks of good decision-making. Good decision-making is a building block of good planning and budgeting. Good planning is a building block of a successful business.

KEY 18

Time series forecasting: the past as prologue

The purpose of forecasting is to try to predict the future. A common forecasting approach is to assume that history will repeat itself and base the prediction on the past. This is called time series forecasting, building on a data set collected or observed over successive increments of time. For example, sales for 24 consecutive months would be a time series. There are three basic models used in time series forecasting: naïve, moving average and smoothing.

A time series forecast makes two basic assumptions. First, the forecasted series is stable and historical data can be used to make accurate predictions. Second, historical data contains information and noise. The information component is the stable repeated pattern that can be used to predict the future. The noise component, while sometimes appearing as a pattern, reflects random fluctuations that contain no predictive ability. A major problem in time series forecasting is properly separating the useful information from the misleading noise. The appropriate time series forecasting method depends on the ratio of information to noise in the historical data.

Naïve models assume that very little information is contained in the time series and that it is mostly noise. Because of the low information content the forecast is heavily based on the most recent data. An example of a naïve-forecasting model is:

$$\hat{Y}_{t+1} = Y_t$$

The forecast for period $t + 1$ is the actual value for period t. Using this model, monthly sales for February would be January's sales. This model is called a random walk and assumes that the time series contains no information. It could be modified to incorporate some information. For example, we could assume that the series is not stationary. The naïve model can incorporate the trend by including the difference between this period and the last period.

$$\hat{Y}_{t+1} = Y_t + (Y_t - Y_{t-1})$$

Moving average models assume that the time series contains information as well as noise. The information component is represented by a smooth wave that reflects how the series changes over time. It is difficult to observe the smooth wave because of random movement caused by the noise. Moving averages smooth the data in order to remove the noise. A three-month moving average uses the average of three months worth of data.

Month	Jan	Feb	Mar	Apr	May	Jun	Jul	Aug	Sep
Sales	$75	$90	$105	$150	$160	$165	$155	$140	$110

$Y_{1-3} = (\$75 + \$90 + \$105)/3 = \$90$, April forecast
$Y_{2-4} = (\$90 + \$105 + \$150)/3 = \$115$, May forecast

$Y_{3-5} = (\$105 + \$150 + \$160)/3 = \$138$, June forecast
$Y_{4-6} = (\$150 + \$160 + \$165)/3 = \$158$, July forecast
$Y_{5-7} = (\$160 + \$165 + \$155)/3 = \$160$, August forecast
$Y_{6-8} = (\$165 + \$155 + \$140)/3 = \$153$, September forecast
$Y_{7-9} = (\$155 + \$140 + \$110)/3 = \$90$, October forecast

The forecaster decides on how many periods are included in the moving average. The smaller the number, the greater the influence of recent observations. An alternative approach referred to as exponential smoothing uses all of the data to prepare the forecast.

Exponential smoothing updates the average of all past data for new observations. The model contains a dampening factor to reflect the forecaster's opinion on the relative information content of more recent observations.

$$\hat{Y}_{t+1} = aY_t + (1-a)\hat{Y}_t$$
or
$$\hat{Y}_{t+1} = \hat{Y}_t + a(Y_t - \hat{Y}_t)$$

This says that the forecast for period $t+1$ is equal to the actual value for period t multiplied by a forecaster determined weight, plus the previous period's forecast multiplied by one minus the weight. It also says that the forecast for period $t+1$ is the forecast for period t plus the weight multiplied by the forecast error for period t. The following example shows an exponential smoothing forecast assuming a weight of 0.40.

Month	Jan	Feb	Mar	Apr	May	Jun	Jul	Aug
Actual sales	$210	$180	$315	$300	$425	$510	$385	$295
Forecasted sales		$210	$198	$245	$267	$330	$402	$395

$Y_{Feb} = \$210 =$ Actual for January
$Y_{Mar} = \$210 + (.40)(\$180 - \$210) = \$198$ forecast for March
$Y_{Apr} = \$198 + (.40)(\$315 - \$198) = \$245$ forecast for April

$Y_{May} = \$245 + (.40)(\$300 - \$245) = \$267$ forecast for May
$Y_{Jun} = \$267 + (.40)(\$425 - \$267) = \$330$ forecast for June
$Y_{Jul} = \$330 + (.40)(\$510 - \$330) = \$402$ forecast for July
$Y_{Aug} = \$402 + (.40)(\$385 - \$402) = \$395$ forecast for August

Several features of the exponential smoothing model are shown in the above example. First, the dampening factor has a value between zero and one. A value of zero puts no weight on the current observation while a value of one puts no weight on the previous forecast. The example uses a weight of 0.40 that places approximately equal weight on the last observation and the previous forecast. Second, the model has to assume a value for the first forecast. In the example the previous observation was used as the forecast. Third, the simple exponential smoothing model shown above provides a constant forecast for all future values of the time series. In cases where a trend or seasonal pattern is present the model must be modified.

Time series techniques such as the moving average and exponential smoothing models are attempts to predict the future value of a variable such as sales using past observations. No one claims that either of these models will fit all forecasting situations. Both methods have two serious limitations. First, even when the forecast is to be based on past observations the data set may require a more customized model. Second, the information contained in the historical data can usually be improved upon by incorporating other information.

KEY 19

Regression: a straight line to better forecasting

A fundamental rule in decision-making is that better information leads to better decisions. Time series models do a good job of processing the information contained in a variable's past observations. But they ignore any information contained in related series. For example, the forecast of direct labor costs would probably improve by incorporating data on production. Regression models can improve time series forecast by including the information from related series.

Regression models are based on the concept of correlation. Correlation is the statistical tendency of one series to move with another and is demonstrated using the following direct labor and production data.

Month	Jan	Feb	Mar	Apr	May	Jun	Jul	Aug	Sep
Direct labor hrs	250	375	525	680	930	530	710	845	455
Units produced	1,200	1,950	2,875	3,600	6,800	1,500	1,625	5,415	1,875

The level of correlation between direct labor hours and units of production is measured using the coefficient of correlation. The coefficient of correlation has values between plus and minus one. A plus one means that the two series move together perfectly. A minus one means that the two series move opposite each other. The coefficient of correlation for the above series is 0.84. This means that direct labor and production are closely related.

Correlation analysis is useful in identifying related series but it is not an adequate forecasting method by itself. Regression analysis is the preferred forecasting technique. It measures the value of one series based on the value of the other series. If we were interested in forecasting direct labor hours using the above data the regression model would be:

$$\text{Direct labor hours} = \alpha + \beta$$
(Units produced)

Direct labor hours is referred to as the dependent variable, α is the number of direct labor hours forecasted when no units are produced, β translates forecasted production into direct labor hours. Based on the above data the regression equation is:

$$\text{Predicted direct labor hours} = 306 + 0.095$$
(Units produced)

According to the regression model, production of 2,500 units would require 543.5 direct labor hours. This is called a point forecast. It provides a forecast but does not convey any level of confidence in the prediction. A confidence interval can be constructed using the output from the regression model. For example, if 2,500 units are produced we can be 95% sure that actual direct labor hours will be between 285 and 802.

The formula for the confidence interval is:

Predicted direct labor hours ± 2
(standard error of the forecast)

In this example the standard error of the forecast is 129.43. The regression results were generated using Excel's regression function.

Sometimes multiple series are used in the regression model. In the following example we want to forecast direct labor hours using units produced and the number of employees involved.

Month	Jan	Feb	Mar	Apr	May	Jun	Jul	Aug	Sep
Direct labor hrs	250	375	525	680	930	530	710	845	455
Units produced	1,200	1,950	2,875	3,600	6,800	1,500	1,625	5,415	1,875
# of employees	25	28	42	51	66	55	57	58	50

Direct labor hours =
$\alpha + \beta_1$ (Units produced) + β_2 (No. of employees)

Using Excel's regression function we obtain the following results:

Predicted direct labor hours =
$-34 + 0.0526$ (Units produced) + 9.71 (No. of employees)

According to the regression output, to produce 2.500 units using 48 employees would require 563.5 direct labor hours. We can be 95% confident that actual direct labor hours will be between 543 and 698. The confidence interval has a smaller range because including the number of employees reduces the standard error of prediction to 67.30.

There is nothing prohibiting you from including more variables in the regression model. For forecasting purposes more data is usually better.

However, it takes time and resources to gather an error free data set and the forecaster must decide if the additional costs are justified.

Regression analysis is a useful forecasting technique. It can also be used to control and direct current operations. Assume that the marketing manager is trying to decide if the advertising effort for a new product should consider the average annual income of potential customers. Data was gathered for a similar product and produced the following regression results.

| Sales | 9,800 | 11,300 | 8,200 | 4,300 | 16,750 | 10,025 | 14,300 | 12,000 |
| Income | 45,000 | 65,000 | 54,000 | 31,000 | 70,000 | 58,000 | 67,200 | 61,350 |

Sales = −3,972 + 0.26 (Average annual income)

The results suggest a positive relationship between sales and the consumer's average annual income. This tells us the direction of the relationship but not its strength. The strength of the relationship is indicated by the t-value. The t-value is provided by Excel's regression function and we want a number greater than 2.0. In this example the t-value is 5.14, which suggests a strong relationship between sales and the level of consumer income.

KEY 20

Judgmental forecasting techniques: when numbers are not enough

I n *Introductory Business Forecasting*, Newbold and Bos note that "If you want your forecasts of product sales next month, it may be useful to consult a statistician. If you want to predict what products will be selling in what quantities in your industry in 20 years' time, consult experts in the relevant areas of research and development, corporate strategy, marketing and so on."

Time series and regression forecasting methods are statistical models based on historical data. They assume that relevant, quality data is available and the environment is stable. When these conditions do not hold, judgment should be injected into the forecast. The degree to which judgment is used depends on how much historical data is available, the analyst's opinion of its forecasting ability and the time horizon. Several judgmental or qualitative models have been developed to supplement or replace quantitative forecasting.

The growth curve forecasting method bases long-run projections on two assumptions. First, changes in technology or other structural shifts are ignored. Second, a growth curve is assumed. The growth curve can be flat, a straight line with an up or down trend, or a curve with a changing slope. The selected curve is based on the forecaster's judgment. A simple example of using a growth curve is to forecast sales twenty years from now to be today's sales growing at a constant 5% per year. The assumptions can be altered to reflect more careful analysis by, for instance, building in an adjustment that the growth rate will decrease by 0.1% each year.

The Delphi method forms forecasts based on the opinions of a group of experts. In stage one a questionnaire is sent to the panel of experts. A review team summarizes the responses and sends them back to the experts. The experts can then revise or defend their position and send the results back to the review team in a process that continues until the review team is fully satisfied with the experts' evaluation. A meeting is called and the experts discuss their viewpoints. At the conclusion of the meeting the review team prepares a forecast. The Delphi method can be very time consuming and expensive.

Cross-impact analysis is often used in conjunction with the Delphi method. It attempts to identify and incorporate any apparently unrelated events that could have a significant impact on the forecast. For example, the firm may form a panel of economists and engineers to help forecast the demand for automobiles two decades from now. Cross-impact analysis might identify changing attitudes towards pollution as a significant variable and add sociologists and experts on environmental law to the panel.

Scenario writing involves the writing of several

scripts outlining possible future conditions and ranked according to likelihood. It is really not forecasting, but requires forecasters to focus on the future, providing useful insights.

La Prospective is an interactive forecasting method. It models the future as the interaction of a series of players and events. The players are identified along with their goals, objectives, strategies and tactics. A series of games, using an assumed set of events and participants, are played (modeled). Cross-impact analysis is used to incorporate seemingly unrelated interactions. The resulting scenarios are studied and considered when making long-run forecasts.

Neural networks represent an attempt to incorporate artificial intelligence into the area of forecasting. It is a black-box approach that relies on the "genetic algorithm" to produce accurate forecasts. The forecaster plugs into the computer a large set of examples. The computer produces a test forecast, which is then evaluated for accuracy.

At some point the accuracy of the forecast is considered acceptable and the model is used on new data to produce an actual forecast. This is referred to as "training" the computer. Because conditions change the computer must be periodically "retrained" or the model will become obsolete. One concern that users have with neural networks is that they never see the model and must trust the technique. Another concern is that the computer can be "over-trained." Neural networks are really just elaborate pattern recognition techniques.

For most short-term forecasting problems the quantitative models produce superior results. Judgmental models, however, can be useful when the data, time horizon, or type of question significantly reduces the reliability of the quantitative models.

KEY 21

Evaluating forecasting models: through the looking glass

The purpose of forecasting is to remove some of the uncertainty involved in making decisions based on future events or conditions. It is the information contained in the forecast that reduces uncertainty. Unfortunately, information is not free. Managers recognize the tradeoff between information and uncertainty. They expend significant amounts of money and time to increase the quality of the information provided by the forecasts.

The higher the quality of the information contained in the forecast the better the quality of the forecast. We can measure the quality of a forecast by measuring its forecasting accuracy. The question then becomes: How do we measure forecast accuracy?

One approach is to focus on the forecasting model. Some managers look at the complexity of the forecasting technique and assume that more complex models will produce more accurate forecasts. A second approach is to focus on the theory and assumptions used to develop the forecasting model. The more reasonable and realistic the theory and assumptions, the more accurate the forecasts. A third approach is to use historical data to generate a test forecast and compare it to the test data. The more closely the test forecast predicts the test data the higher its quality. Probably the best approach is to make a forecast, wait for the future to arrive and compare forecasted and actual results. You can then refine the forecasting techniques for future use.

Better quality information produces more accurate, higher quality forecasts. But while the quality of a forecast is important, time and money are also important. Firms cannot afford to devote unlimited resources to the forecasting process and some sort of accuracy-cost tradeoff policy must be established.

The policy should address three issues. First, a cost function must be developed that allows managers to estimate the cost of acquiring additional information. Second, the relationship between the incremental information and improvements in forecasting accuracy must be identified. Third, managers must be able to translate incremental improvements in forecasting accuracy into increases in firm value.

The first step in evaluating a forecasting method is to measure its predictive ability. Predictive ability or accuracy is measured by the model's prediction error. The prediction or forecast error is defined as (Actual − Forecast). In principle, the lower the forecast error the higher the quality of the forecast. The following three measures are frequently used to measure a forecasting technique's accuracy. The first is the mean absolute error (MAE). MAE doesn't care whether the forecast was high or low, just that it differed from actual results. The formula for the mean absolute error (MAE) is:

$$\text{MAE} = \frac{\sum_{t+1}^{n} \left| Y_t - \hat{Y}_t \right|}{n}$$

There are n observations. Y_t is the actual value for observation t and $\hat{Y}_t$ is the predicted value.

The second measure is the mean absolute prediction error (MAPE). It expresses MAE as a percent of the quantity being measured. The formula for the mean absolute prediction error (MAPE) is:

$$\text{MAPE} = \frac{\sum_{t+1}^{n} 100 \left| Y_t - \hat{Y}_t \right|}{n Y_t}$$

The third measure is the mean squared error (MSE). The MSE is basically the variance of the forecast error. The formula for the mean squared error is:

$$\text{MSE} = \frac{\sum_{t+1}^{n} \left(Y_t - \hat{Y}_t \right)^2}{n}$$

MSE can be difficult to interpret because it is expressed in squared units. The root mean square error (RMSE) improves the interpretation of the MSE by expressing the results in same units as the quantity being measured. The formula for the root mean square error (RMSE) is:

$$\text{RMSE} = \sqrt{\sum_{t=1}^{n} \left(Y_t - \hat{Y}_t \right)^2 \Big/ n}$$

The following example shows how these measures are used to judge forecasting accuracy.

Time	1	2	3	4	5	6	7	8	9
Forecast	28	17	40	51	48	66	69	70	75
Actual	25	19	33	52	45	63	67	74	81

MAE = (|25–28| + |19–17| + |33–40| + |52–51| + |45–48| +
|63–66| + |67–69| + |74–70| + |81–75|)/9 = 3.44

MAPE = (|25–28|/25 + |19–17| /19 + |33–40|/33 + |52–51|
/52 + |45–48|/45 + |63–66|/63 + |67–69|/67 +
|74–70|/74 + |81–75|/81)(100/9) = 8.1

The MAPE says that the forecasting technique being used is generating prediction errors that on average are 8.1% of the quantity being forecasted. It is probably the most easily understood because it is not sensitive to the units of the forecasted variable.

MSE = [$(25–28)^2$ + $(19–17)^2$ + $(33–40)^2$ + $(52–51)^2$ +
$(45–48)^2$ + $(63–66)^2$ + $(67–69)^2$ + $(74–70)^2$ +
$(81–75)2]/9 = 15.22$

$$RMSE = 15.22^{1/2} = 3.90$$

RMSE is basically the standard deviation of the forecast. It says that, on average, the forecast misses the actual value by 3.90 units. The MAE and RMSE are similar except that the RMSE is based on squared deviations instead of absolute deviations. This allows the RMSE to penalize large forecast errors more heavily than small errors.

If you are only concerned with the accuracy of the forecast the preferred technique is the one with the smallest value for the selected evaluation measure. Sometimes, however, it is important to express the magnitude of the forecast in terms of the cost associated with the error. In this case the cost of an error must be measured by developing a cost function that translates the error into a dollar amount. The quadratic cost function (QCF) is the most popular. It specifies the cost of a forecast error of any amount to be proportional to the squared error. Assume that, in the above example, the firm specified the quadratic cost function to be $125 times the forecast error squared.

The QCF is calculated as follows:

$$QCF = \$125 \; [(25-28)^2 + (19-17)^2 + (33-40)^2 + (52-51)^2 + (45-48)^2 + (63-66)^2 + (67-69)^2 + (74-70)^2 + (81-75)^2]/9 = \$1,902.50$$

There are many ways to evaluate a forecasting method. The above techniques represent the most popular, but they don't fit every situation. The most appropriate technique will depend on the problem.

KEY 22

Financial models: the black boxes of planning

Financial models, sometimes referred to as corporate financial models, are part of a firm's management information system (MIS). An important part of the financial model is the budget. It models the company's physical and financial operations, summarizes strategies and activities, and projects the outcome. Since the budget is a model and models are abstractions from reality, it is only as good as the underlying assumptions and decisions that it incorporates.

The firm's planning and budget process depends on the quality of the underlying decisions. The better the decision-making process, the greater the chances that the firm will achieve its goals and objectives. Financial models were developed to help managers make better decisions and no model should be adopted that doesn't meet that criterion.

It is important to understand that a financial model is an aid, not a replacement for good decision-making skills. Even with modern computers and

Soon gotten, soon spent;

ill gotten, ill spent.

John Heywood

modeling software decision-making is still difficult and challenging. Indeed, as the planning process proceeds it is important to keep track of what information is known and what events are still uncertain. Most corporate financial models are based on the assumption that their primary function is to provide more information. Managers need relevant information, but many financial models generate irrelevant information. An effective corporate financial model should filter and condense the information into useful packages.

It is generally assumed that more information improves the manager's decision-making and planning. But it is easy to drown under information overload. The plans may be designed to meet multiple objectives and progress toward one may impede progress toward another. Decision-makers may see the problem from different perspectives. For example, they may disagree on the level or form of uncertainty involved or they may disagree about the value of a particular outcome. The financial model should be designed to consider these issues and provide managers with a manageable set of decisions.

The design of the firm's financial model must identify each important type of financial decision that will be addressed by the model, and the interactions between them. This includes not only financial decisions already made, but also decisions not made because of inadequate resources, computing power or software. Recent computer hardware and software advances make it possible to address previously unsolvable issues.

The financial model must be capable of handling different types of problems. Some problems can be structured so that the model can find an optimal solution. These problems usually contain no uncertainty and can be solved using analytic models. Analytic models, also referred to as optimization models, consist of mathematical equations that can generate an optimal output when given proper inputs. For example, analytic models are used to determine a firm's optimal inventory level.

Many problems, however, are difficult or impossible to solve using an optimization model. For example, consider a situation where customers can freely switch between products. In this case it is impossible to predict sales with certainty. Simulation models work well on this type of problem. Simulation models, also called Monte-Carlo models, are computer models that imitate a real life situation. These models do not produce a single optimal solution. Instead they produce a distribution of alternative solutions, and give the probability of each solution. Simulation models are often used to determine how sensitive results are to changes in inputs. For example, sensitivity analysis can be used to determine the impact on sales of a product when the price is increased or decreased by ten percent.

In many cases the approximate answers produced by simulation models are very close to the answer provided by the analytic model. For example, assume that a simulation model simulated flipping a coin 1,000 times and produced heads 50.9% of the time. This is an estimate of the probability of flipping a coin and getting a head. An analytic model would show mathematically that the probability of getting a head was exactly 50%. The approximate nature of simulation models means that no matter how many times we simulated the coin flip we could never be sure that we had the correct answer. Analytic models have the advantage that they provide exact answers, but they are more difficult to model and not as easy to understand.

There is a third class of problem where uncertainty cannot be modeled with probabilities. This class of problem occurs when the optimal decision depends on the decisions made by other individuals after they observe your decision. For example, whether or not to reduce the sales price for your product depends on how the competition reacts. The optimal decision depends on how others are expected to react. Decision tree and influence diagram models are particularly useful in solving this class of problem.

Still, no matter how powerful models become as computers become more advanced, managers will never be able to escape their responsibility to monitor the system and make modifications or updates.

KEY 23

Financial modeling: spreadsheets and add-ins

Computers and sophisticated software packages have become part of every financial model. Spreadsheet packages like Microsoft Excel or Lotus 1-2-3 allow managers to develop models using databases, mathematical equations, and logic operators that specify the relationships among variables. The example (shown on next page) shows how Excel can be used to develop a sales budget.

Product A's unit sales are forecasted for each quarter of 1999. Quarterly unit sales for 2000 are estimated to be 15% higher than unit sales for the respective quarter in 1999. Sales price per unit is forecasted to increase by a constant one percent per quarter. Total sales are the product of unit sales and sales price.

Product B's unit sales are forecasted for each quarter of 1999. Quarterly unit sales for the first two quarters of 2000 are estimated to be 10% higher than unit sales for the respective quarter in

1999. Unit sales for quarters three and four are forecasted to be 15% higher than their respective 1999 quarters. Sales price per unit is forecasted to be $2.50 for 1999 and $2.75 for 2000. Total sales are the product of unit sales and sales price. Since only one input value is provided for each variable we can assume that the variables can be measured with certainty.

XYZ Co. Sales Budget				
For the two year period ending December 31, 2000				
1999	1	2	3	4
Product A				
Unit sales	500	800	1,500	2,000
Sales price	$15	$15.15	$15.30	$15.45
Total sales	$7,500	$12,120	$22,952	$30,909
Product B				
Unit Sales	2,500	2,250	1,700	1,500
Sales Price	$2.50	$2.50	$2.50	$2.50
Total Sales	$6,250	$5,625	$4,250	$3,750
2000	1	2	3	4
Product A				
Unit sales	575	920	1725	2300
Sales price	$15.61	$15.77	$15.92	$16.08
Total sales	$8,975	$14,504	$27,467	$36,989
Product B				
Unit sales	2750	2475	1955	1725
Sales price	$2.75	$2.75	$2.75	$2.75
Total sales	$7,563	$6,806	$5,376	$4,744
Total sales for 1999 and 2000				$205,780

Excel and Lotus contain functions that allow us to prepare optimization or analytic models. For example, assume that the firm faces a production capacity constraint. Each quarter in 1999 it can produce a maximum of 1,750 units of product A and 2,700 units of product B. In 2000 the maximum quarterly production is 2,100 units for product A and 2,700 units for product B. The firm is limited to a maximum yearly production of 6,300 units of product A and 8,200 units of product B. Because the same equipment is used to produce both products total quarterly production is limited to 3,700 units.

Solver is an Excel add-in that allows us to determine the maximum profit that can be achieved with the given data and production constraints. Solver produced the following results.

1999	1	2	3	4
Product A				
Unit sales	1050	1750	1,750	1,750
Sales price	$15	$15.15	$15.30	$15.45
Total quarterly sales: A	$15,750	$26,513	$26,778	$27,045
Product B				
Unit sales	2,650	1,950	1,900	1,700
Sales price	$2.50	$2.50	$2.50	$2.50
Total quarterly sales: B	$6,625	$4,875	$4,750	$4,250
Unit sales A&B	3,700	3,700	3,650	3,450
Total quarterly sales: A & B	$22,375	$31,388	$31,528	$31,295

2000	1	2	3	4
Product A				
Unit sales	700	1400	2100	2100
Sales price	$15.61	$15.77	$15.92	$16.08
Total quarterly sales: A	$10,926	$22,071	$33,438	$33,772
Product B				
Unit sales	2700	2300	1600	1600
Sales price	$2.75	$2.75	$2.75	$2.75
Total quarterly sales: B	$7,425	$6,325	$4,400	$4,400
Unit sales A&B	3,400	3,700	3,700	3,700
Total quarterly sales: A & B	$18,351	$28,396	$37,838	$38,172

Total Sales for 1999 and 2000				$239,343

Given the production constraints and sales price, maximum total sales for the two year period is $239,343. This spreadsheet did not incorporate any uncertainty about the level of unit sales. To modify the example to incorporate uncertain sales, you can use a probability distribution, which lists possible values for a variable along with the chance that a given value will occur.

Assume that quarterly sales are uncertain but that they have the following probability distribution.

1999	1	2	3	4
Product A Unit Sales				
30%	900	1,500	1,500	1,500
50%	1,150	1,800	1,800	1,800
20%	1,025	2,000	2,000	2,000
Product B Unit Sales				
.10	2,300	2,000	900	1,500
.50	2,200	2,200	2,000	1,000
.40	2,925	2,375	1,525	2,125

2000	1	2	3	4
Product A Unit Sales				
30%	800	1,600	1,800	1,800
50%	500	1,400	2,500	2,500
20%	1050	1,100	1,550	1,550
Product B Unit Sales				
0.1	2,200	1,800	1,800	1,350
0.5	3,000	2,190	1,790	1,880
0.4	2,575	3,000	2,200	1,625

A popular Excel add-in sold by Palisade Corporation called @RISK is used to incorporate the probability distribution for unit sales.

1999	1	2	3	4
Product A				
Distribution of unit sales				
30%	900	1,500	1,500	1,500
50%	1,150	1,800	1,800	1,800
20%	1,025	2,000	2,000	2,000
Unit sales	1,025	1,800	1,800	1,800
Sales price	$15	$15.15	$15.30	$15.45
Sales revenue A	$15,375	$27,270	$27,543	$27,818
Product B				
Distribution of unit sales				
0.1	2,300	2,000	900	1,500
0.5	2,200	2,200	2,000	1,000
0.4	2,925	2,375	1,525	2,125
Unit sales	2,300	2,200	1,525	1,500
Sales price	$2.50	$2.50	$2.50	$2.50
Sales revenue B	$5,750	$5,500	$3,813	$3,750
Sales revenue A&B	$21,125	$32,770	$31,355	$31,568

2000	1	2	3	4
Product A				
Distribution of unit sales				
30%	800	1,600	1,800	1,800
50%	500	1,400	2,500	2,500
20%	1050	1,100	1,550	1,550
Sales price	$15.45	$15.61	$15.77	$15.92
Sales revenue A	$12,364	$21,853	$28,377	$28,661
Product B				
Distribution of unit sales				
0.1	2,200	1,800	1,800	1,350
0.5	3,000	2,190	1,790	1,880
0.4	2,575	3,000	2,200	1,625
Unit sales	2,575	2,190	1,800	1,625
Sales price	$2.75	$2.75	$2.75	$2.75
Sales revenue B	$7,081	$6,023	$4,950	$4,469
Sales revenue A&B	$19,445	$27,875	$33,327	$33,130
Total Revenue				$230,595

@RISK calculates summary statistics and the distribution of "Total Revenue."

Minimum =	213686.5	5% =	222980.6	55% =	239916.3
Maximum =	266868.4	10% =	225805.5	60% =	240645.7
Mean =	239664.8	15% =	229196	65% =	242499.5
Std deviation =	10270.25	20% =	230457.9	70% =	244306.9
Variance =	1.05E+08	25% =	233034.5	75% =	245466.9
Skewness =	0.1908308	30% =	234697.6	80% =	247993.4
Kurtosis =	2.873518	35% =	235663.3	85% =	251224.1
Mode =	237943.3	40% =	236814.3	90% =	252985.2
		45% =	237987.6	95% =	257733.1
		50% =	238626.2		

According to the @RISK analysis there is a 50% chance, given the above data, that total revenue for the next two years will be greater than $238,626. @RISK also produced the following probability distribution for "Total Revenue." The graph provides information about the probability of getting "Total Revenue" values other than the mean of $238,626.

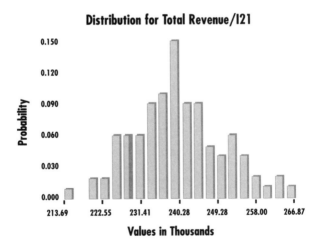

Distribution for Total Revenue/I21

KEY 24

Financial modeling: more on spreadsheets and add-ins

Consider the range of decisions the budgeting and planning process requires of managers. Which product lines should be continued? How much should be produced and what inventory levels should be maintained? What is the optimal level and form of liquidity? Which capital projects should be selected?

Analytic models were developed first to help answer these kinds of questions. They work well under conditions of certainty and their major advantage is that they can find exact optimal solutions. Their major disadvantages are that they do not work well when conditions are uncertain.

The second step in the evolution of these techniques was the development of simulation models. These models are much more flexible and can solve a much larger set of problems. But they provide only approximate answers and they don't incorporate sequential decision-making.

The third step was the development of decision trees and influence diagrams. Several software packages such as DPL (Decision Programming Language) and Precision Tree by Palisade Corporation incorporate both decision trees and influence diagrams.

A decision tree analyzes a problem by graphing it using different nodes consisting of decision points or outcomes.

The following example uses Precision Tree to demonstrate how decision trees can help prepare budgets. A decision must be made whether to produce Product A or Product B. The initial startup costs for Product A is $375,000; for Product B it is $400,000. Both products have a two-year life.

Product A has the following properties: There is a 50% chance that demand will be high, leading to sales revenue of $110,000. There is an equal 50% chance that year one sales will only be $30,000. The probability distribution of sales in year two depends on sales in year one. If sales in year one are high, there is an 85%chance that sales in year two will be $845,000 and a 15% chance that year two sales will be $262,000. However if year one sales are low then there is a 40% chance that year two sales will be $773,000 and a 60% chance that year two sales will be $115,000.

There is a 60% chance that year one demand for Product B will be high in year one, producing sales revenue of $91,000, and a 40% chance that year one sales will only be $50,000. If year one sales are high, there is a 75% chance that year two sales will be $33,000 and a 25% chance that they will be $157,000. Low year one sales changes the probability distribution of year two sales to a 30% chance of being $184,000 and a 70% of $83,000.

According to the decision tree Product B is the better choice. The optimal choice follows the "True" branches of the tree. The "False" branches should not be selected. Total expected sales, including the $400,000 initial startup costs, are $238,000.

The example could be extended to include additional features such as flexibility options. Flexibility options might include the option to cease production of either product after the first year or the

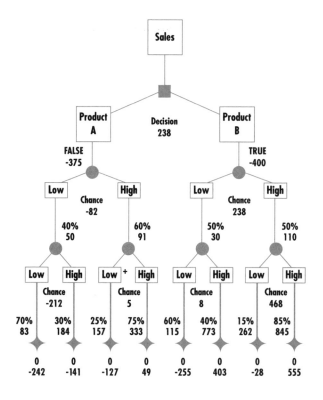

option to increase production if first year sales are high. These are valuable options and should be included in the analysis. Decision trees give managers the ability to incorporate into the model separate but related decisions made at different points in time. The problem is that they can quickly grow to an unmanageable size. It is common for decision trees to have thousands of branches. Influence diagrams were developed to solve the size problem while maintaining the structure.

Recently the decision tree and simulation models have been combined into a new technique called "stochastic decision tree" analysis. This approach allows managers to use more complex probability distributions, model more complex problems and incorporate the decision-maker's attitude toward risk. Advances in computing power and software have made it possible for managers to plan and budget using decisions based on the output from very sophisticated financial models.

KEY 25

Profit-making firms can learn from nonprofit organizations

The goal of profit-oriented firms is to maximize owner's wealth. Sales are the primary instrument for such firms and the planning and budgeting process usually starts with a sales forecast. Nonprofit organizations, on the other hand, generally do not generate sales. Their mission is to provide certain services with available resources. For example, a school district may receive revenue from the state to maintain and operate the school system. In this case the district's objective is to allocate the funds to provide the maximum services. In this situation the budget itself becomes the central planning tool. In fact, for many nonprofit organizations the budget is so important that it becomes law. The business manager of a school district once remarked that the easiest way for him to break the law was to spend more or less than called for in the budget. Because of its importance, nonprofit organizations have developed budgeting techniques that should be adopted by for-profit firms.

Nonprofit organizations developed the flexible chart of accounts in response to their need to carefully manage spending. The flexible chart of accounts is a useful cost accounting and budget tool that has been adopted by many for-profit firms. The following is an example of how one would be prepared.

Account	Account Number
Assets	
Cash	100.000 – 100.999
Marketable securities	101.000 – 101.999
Accounts receivable	102.000 – 102.999
Equipment	110.000 – 110.999
Buildings	150.000 – 150.999
Liabilities	
Accounts payable	200.000 – 200.999
Wages payable	201.000 – 201.999
Short-term debt	210.000 – 210.999
Long-term debt	250.000 – 250.000
Owner's Equity	
Common stock	270.000 – 270.999
Retained earnings	280.000 – 280.999
Income	
Sales	300.000 – 300.999
Other revenue	310.000 – 310.000
Expenses	
Cost of goods sold	
Raw materials	401.000 – 401.999
Direct labor	402.000 – 402.999
Direct overhead	403.000 – 403.999
Other expenses	450.000 – 450.999

In the above example, the first digit represents where the item appeared in the financial statements: asset, liability, equity, revenue and expense. The second digit represents the major category of each item and the third digit represents the specific category. The three digits after the decimal place are used for individual categories, such as receivables from commercial customers or receivables from government customers.

The value of the flexible chart of accounts is that costs can be classified and summarized, and cost accounting reports can be quickly generated using available accounting software packages. It not only improves the ability of the firm to control costs, it also forces managers to consider the relationship among various accounts.

The flexible chart of account can also be linked to cost or revenue centers. For example, the report for Store A might look like this:

	Store A: No. 884	
	Account	Amount
300.100.884	Sales	$1,450,000
300.110.884	Discount sales	650,000
300.500.884	Other sales	75,000
300.***.884	Total sales	$2,175,000
401.100.884	Sporting goods purchases	$350,000
401.200.884	Automotive purchases	285,000
401.300.884	Apparel purchases	477,000
401.***.884	Total purchases	$1,112,000

It is important that expenditures for nonprofit organizations do not exceed the budget. In some cases this is a violation of the law that can result in serious penalties. Therefore, the organization needs to know not only the amount of budgeted funds already spent, but also the amount of any outstanding purchase orders for goods or services that have not been received or billed. In order to control these costs nonprofit organizations encumber funds when they are committed. For example, a typical for-profit firm would not make an accounting entry until goods were received and billed, but the nonprofit organization would adjust the budget to record the funds as encumbered.

Many for-profit firms encumber budget items to show that they have, in effect, already been spent. This can be especially useful for firms with spending limits dictated by contracts. If the contractor exceeds the limit the customer will not reimburse them. By reducing the budget when funds are committed instead of when they are received and billed, the contractor can ensure that spending limits are not exceeded.

A simple procedure for encumbering funds is to reduce the budget whenever a purchase order is prepared. A copy is sent to the supplier, a copy is sent to accounts payable, and a copy is sent to the budget department. The department preparing the purchase order keeps a copy and the budget department makes an accounting entry reducing the budget for encumbered funds.

Because spending according to the budget is so important for nonprofit organizations, they have devoted more effort than many for-profit firms to budget management. For-profit firms should consider adopting the practices of preparing a flexible chart of accounts and formally encumbering funds.

INDEX

AUTHOR

NORMAN H. MOORE, Ph.D., is an Associate Professor of Finance at the University of Connecticut, Storrs. He has taught at the graduate MBA, graduate EMBA and undergraduate levels. He has served as President and CEO of Systronics, Inc., where he oversaw design, development and implementation of accounting/financial information applications for stand-alone and timeshare computer systems, and has presented seminars on Treasury Management and Performance Measurement for Commercial Banks and Derivatives Regulation in the U.S. in the Philippines and the People's Republic of China.